SOLDIER BOX

SOLDIER BOX

WHY I WON'T RETURN
TO THE WAR ON TERROR

JOE GLENTON

VERSO
London • New York

First published by Verso 2013
© Joe Glenton 2013

1 3 5 7 9 10 8 6 4 2

Verso
UK: 6 Meard Street, London W1F 0EG
US: 20 Jay Street, Suite 1010, Brooklyn, NY 11201

www.versobooks.com

Verso is the imprint of New Left Books

ISBN-13: 978-1-78168-092-6

British Library Cataloguing in Publication Data
A catalogue record for this book is available from the British Library

Library of Congress Cataloging-in-Publication Data
Glenton, Joe, 1982–
Soldier box : why I won't return to war / Joe Glenton. – 1st edition.
pages cm
ISBN 978-1-78168-092-6 (hbk. : alk. paper)
1. Glenton, Joe, 1982- 2. Afghan War, 2001–Desertions–Great Britain.
3. Military deserters–Great Britain–Biography 4. Conscientious objectors–Great
Britain–Biography. 5. Soldiers–Great Britain–Biography. 6. Soldiers–Political
activity–Great Britain. 7. Afghan War, 2001–Participation, British. 8. Afghan War,
2001–Personal narratives. I. Title. II. Title: Why I won't return to war.
DS371.413.G64 2013
958.104'78–dc23
[B]
2013002226

Typeset in Fournier by MJ & N Gavan, Truro, Cornwall
Printed and bound by CPI Group (UK) Ltd, Croydon, CR0 4YY

For Jim and for all the wild horses

Introduction: Remand, 2009

It's December. I've been put in prison for opposing the war in Afghanistan. Lots of other people disagree with it, lots of people think it is variously a stupid or illegal or unjustified or doomed war. The problem is that I am not supposed to say these things because I am a soldier; and yet I keep saying them.

Remand is when you are held in prison awaiting trial. Sometimes it is for those considered a flight risk and at other times it is for those not yet tried and convicted but considered too dangerous to be out in the world – I belong to the latter category. What I have said damages the 'war effort' and I have said it with that intention. Remand is purgatory.

They tell us it's not a prison, but we can't go out. We're held in a centre for corrections. I find irony in that idea and in the idea that the individuals who've sent me here actually believe it is me who needs adjustment. The Military Correctional Training Centre (MCTC) claims to improve soldiers or discharge them as good citizens. To me it's a funny idea – funny ha-ha, and funny strange.

I share my room in the remand wing with three others. It is here that we play cards at a table in the centre of the room. The others are regularly distracted by reality television, which they love and I hate equally. Summers comes from a

Scottish regiment. I knew him briefly at the Defence School of Transport when he had been a trainee vehicle mechanic. He later switched trades to the infantry and now he has an Afghan medal, three counts of AWOL (five, eight and 133 days) and post-traumatic stress disorder. In line with unofficial tri-service policy, it would not be diagnosed, treated or taken into account for his court martial, despite his history and symptoms. After returning from a harrowing six months in Helmand he drowned himself in drink and drugs. His teenage girlfriend and his parents had posted him as a missing person when he disappeared for several days, sleeping off some chemical stupor. His unit posted him AWOL. Returning to duty, he claims, his sergeant major told him not to go sick with his condition because mental illness ruins careers.

Tommy is an Ulsterman. He has an English father and an Ulster-born mother and claims he is a militant. He talks passionately about flute bands – which he pronounces flute 'bohnds' – and paramilitaries like Johnny Adair and 'Top Gun' McKeag. He is heavily tattooed and has a star inked underneath one eye that signifies an illicit deed carried out for the paramilitaries. He is in the logistics corps, like me. Tommy has attracted charges for ABH, AWOL, Drunkenness and Stealing a German Army General's Bicycle While Drunk. In between playing hands of Shithead, Tommy draws vibrant loyalist images on the back of a notepad: A5 sectarian murals, like the sides of tiny Irish houses. He flips it over occasionally to tally scores.

Trevor is the final player. He is small, muscular and loud. He argues with the screws at every opportunity and is the serial door-kicker during lockdown. He is a Kingsman (a private in the Duke of Lancaster's Regiment), and is in for AWOL and GBH, which he hopes will be dropped to Affray. He and Summers have shaved their heads completely, and for this crime they have been given extra duties, mopping and buffering the floors with an ancient, unwieldy buffing machine. Regulations say that a grade 2 is the shortest cut allowed without a medical chit.

Summers was a veteran of Afghanistan, Tommy has been there twice and Trevor has done Iraq. Two of them have young children, but these men drift from mature and robust to infantile and mischievous, always irreverent. They talk about shots fired in anger, IEDs, RPGs, ambushes, natives and mortars that missed them and sometimes hit someone else. Near misses and drunken brawling are favourite topics. They laugh often.

They are veterans, sons, parents and thugs. They represent the collected scum of three British nations and their average age is twenty-one. Now they are prisoners on remand. Waiting to be forgiven or reconditioned with or without discharge at the end of it. They are problems to be solved. Men reduced to Ministry of Defence forms.

Life in the military is transient. I will meet Summers briefly again after I am sentenced and sent back here to the prison as a DUS – a detainee under sentence – a convict. The others have become just names and fragmented memories to me. But here for a short time we are still soldiers and so we treat each other in a soldierly fashion. We share tobacco, play cards, nominate people to get the brews and abuse each other verbally. Abuse between soldiers is most often an expression of solidarity; in fact, it's the main expression of solidarity. Soldiers cannot always guarantee an opportunity to die for each other, but they can always rip into each other and this process reinforces the bonds that the army wants to see: men who can say anything to each other and still coexist. The trick is to never bite at someone's abuse, just have a go back or shrug it off. Any other response is weakness and will be rounded upon and must be rounded upon and should be. Never, ever bite when you are baited. This is our culture; the only stable thing in our unsettled lives is that ours is an abusive, masculine and transient world.

I was sent here to be silenced, having performed my own small acts of dissent. My incarceration was malicious revenge from my bumbling superiors for having dragged them through the mud. I have outed them in public, a taboo that breaks all the rules. I have questioned what is going on in Afghanistan and this is my punishment. The military is meant to be a silent leviathan but they have bitten. The ripples my actions have caused ruin the illusion of efficiency, strength and account-ability, and of grim-faced adherence to duty at any cost.

The problem is that as much as they would like to think it, I don't work for them anymore. Nevertheless, I am afraid, as they want to send me down for years – my own officers have assured me of this with confidence. I have a life and I want to get it back. This time on remand will come off any later sentence. But what, I ask myself, if it is years? The charges against me indicate a punishment, which may stretch for tens of years, if they have the balls. The only thing that keeps me playing cards, and not giving in, is my view that I am right to defy them. I am right, they are wrong – fuck them, fuck the toffs and the politicians and the army.

When my fellow prisoners ask me what I'm here for I tell them. Brows furrow. 'Talking to the media? Can you get done for that? That's bullshit, mate, you've been stitched up!' And it's true, this has never happened with regards to Afghanistan: my protest was public and my detention rests within a legal grey area. I argue it is unlawful. But the law here is solely interpreted by my captors to suit their immediate needs. There were once two charges for disobeying orders but these were dropped weeks ago, a judge confirming they were removed in a hearing. There are five more charges being considered. These charges are either dead or not yet born. They don't know what to do with me, because I am attacking them with all the bloody-mindedness they instilled in me and I am doing it well. 'They don't like the sunlight,' my legal man said of the coverage. 'It makes their slime dry up.'

Chapter 1

The first place I remember is a cottage in Norfolk. My father is from a place near there. A place so small it is called Smallburgh. He is a wild-looking giant with a beard. He was dyslexic when the condition was called stupidity and had a head for maths and a penchant for practical things. In those days he was a long-haired, earring-wearing truck driver and this upset my maternal grandmother who didn't send my mother to grammar school in order to bag that kind of man.

My mother is a small, fierce Yorkshirewoman who wandered far from home. After divorcing her alcoholic RAF husband, she and my father met and not long after had my brother and, eighteen months later, me. Though my father tried on their first date, he was rewarded with a slap in a lay-by. A story he still repeats happily and unasked. We lived in Norfolk amid leafy lanes and pretty countryside, until we went north. The move cost us my Norfolk dialect and the price of a truck. We ended up near York, my mother's home.

I outgrew school by the time I was eight years old, the boredom of classrooms and the struggling teachers gave me nothing I wanted. As soon as I left that cage to be home-educated I began to read and write, and have never stopped. I spent those years clutching a book or paper and pencil. I have heard some people suggest that this made me a misfit but sometimes things defy unpacking for having been lived; that's to say I am unsure if my unusual schooling contributed to my decisions.

My brother left school a year later and we lived in our little rural village. I knew no other way. We learned about what interested us, which was everything. The history and nature in the valley formed a foundation for what I love today: the quiet, the rural and the old.

I was a sensitive kid and grew my hair long, feral and scruffy, and I stropped when people mistook me for a girl. I was a little know-it-all until I grew bigger and smarmier, and clever with it. My brother and father were more outdoorsy and robust while I was bookish and introvert from early on. It took me many years to learn to accept the outdoors as they did and later to love it – the cold, the heat, the physical work. I wrote stories and read books about adventure and war and heroes and kept my own company. I tormented my brother with my smart-arse little brother act. With no school there was no sense of hierarchy drilled into me. I would not defer to adults or bigger kids. I sometimes made a point of fighting with the older, stronger kids, and I'd gouge and punch and bite. Although I tried and kept trying to beat them, I almost always lost – but they remembered me.

Once, after we left school, a man from the education authority visited our house to check our progress but we set our cat on him and said nothing as it nestled and moulted white fur on his black suit. This and the written work I had assembled once I left school saw him off. I shuttled piles of filled exercise books down from my room for him to appraise, even as the old tom pawed his lap with predatory eyes. He did not return. My life after this was played out in long summers with no school to hamper my education.

The landlord of our small village was a barrister whose forebears had, allegedly, won the valley in a card game many years before from a drunker, richer, even more bloated landlord. It was here that I first experienced the power of class, though I did not understand those rigid tiers which had shaped my life. The striking thing about the people up on the hill, apart from their utter detachment from reality, was that while wealthy they were stuck trying to keep up with the real aristocracy, the real old money, whom they courted over dinners cooked by my mother.

The most condescending term for the working class would better fit these specimens: aspirational. 'Oh, you're so lucky,' the lady of the manor had once told my mother, betraying her schema, 'you can wear cheap earrings'. They pumped out three long-limbed, horse-faced daughters and finally a son whom they referred to simply as The Boy.

After living there for years we were ejected, homeless. The landlord sacked my father one day for recalcitrance unbearable in a peasant. After my father had explained that he could not be sacked by him because he did not work for him, the barrister sacked my mother more successfully. The experience of being cast out was in keeping with centuries past.

There was a hearing over the eviction, which my mother attended. It did not go unnoticed that the landlord and the judge chatted on first name terms and discussed how hard it was to get 'good domestic staff'. After that we moved from job to job: forestry, farming, even working on a fox hunt in a house next to the pens in which the hounds would sing out the evening. In the hunting season the red-coated toffs would lord it up sipping drinks and haw-hawing astride their hunting horses, while the rural workers would doff their hats to the bastards. As I grew, my dislike of those divisions grew with me. The arrogance of the hunters seemed as inappropriate and odd as the willingness of the hunt followers to defer to these people. After a year or so we moved from the hunt to another town.

For a while I became an army cadet and enjoyed it. It was the only local club that appealed to me and so I spent two evenings a week marching around the tennis courts of a school with a bunch of other cadets and a few weekends away shooting targets and doing field exercises. I won an award for best uniform turnout and told the instructors I wanted to be a marine. That detachment was aligned with an infantry regiment called the Green Howards. We wore their badge in our berets and the instructors tried to persuade me to join that unit. 'Or the corps,' they said, 'the signals, the engineers or some such. Get a trade.' But I left the cadets when hormones started to kick in and took my issued kit with me for good measure.

By the age of fifteen darker times arrived for me and my family. My brother had moved far away to work on a fox-hunt in Devon. He had left at fifteen having acquired a National Insurance number by omission. After he had gone, life carried on the same for a while, until my mother and father split up. Life was hard, we were poor, and this took its toll. My parents argued one day when I was out at a friend's house and my mother rang me there to tell me not to go home. I ended up moving with her to a hostel in another town, where we lived for a few months. Here I started learning how to drink, smoke weed and pop pills.

Eventually my dad left the old house and we moved back in. My mother had developed manic depression and was becoming increasingly erratic in her behaviour. I did not help matters and my spotty, squeaky-voiced adolescent rebellion got me ejected from home. I spent a night sleeping rough before going into care, and ended up back in the pill-popping, weed-smoking town we'd stayed in briefly – only now I was living in sheltered accommodation.

Rural Yorkshire was a place without provisions; the main job prospects were the dreaded Baco, the local bacon factory. Our lives were dominated by fighting with each other, trying to snare girls, talking about fighting, and seeing how many drugs our giros could buy while not starving. A few people I knew joined the army and I thought that this might be a good idea too, and then binned it. The drugs and hijinks were much more compelling at that age.

As I started to spiral out of control I had gathered a gang of miscreant, small-town friends – some of whom are now dead or in prison. We once went to a neighbouring town in search of adventure. But after an evening of the usual chavvish revelry, matters became fraught. Our de facto leader Fried Aaron pointed out that Dodgy Barry, another of our number, was renowned and had been banned from that town. In order to get rid of him, we went to the police station hoping for a lift back, but no one was there, just an unmanned phone. We rang it and the operator helpfully told us that there were no police in the area. With there being no police we decided to nick a car. Finding a Vauxhall Nova down an alley, we got it open but managed to snap the locked steering wheel with a metal bar. Having failed in this endeavour, we fled and decided to hike back the ten miles or so cross-country. Between the two towns lay Flamingo Land, a theme park and zoo. As we crossed ditches and climbed fences, great, black, steaming shapes closed in around us. We had stumbled into an enclosure full of buffalo it seemed. We fled again and made it back as the sun came up. In those shitty little towns this was the kind of stuff we did to pass the time. Our lives were full of bullshit talk about what we were going to do, and how we would escape, but very few of us did.

I fled that town owing money for pills and got my first job as a live-in waiter in a posh hotel near Rievaulx. The novelty of minimum-wage labour faded quickly. Our clientele varied between wealthy, tweed-clad shooting parties, American retirees, and so on. Not having been shaped by teachers and school hierarchies, I saw no reason to hold my tongue, and I was constantly in trouble for answering back to the management. This job lasted a few months until I got bored. By this time my mother had been sectioned and released and was beginning to recover. Meanwhile I ended up in another hostel in Norfolk. I met a girl there and we moved in together. I took up kickboxing and fell in love with it, becoming teetotal for those years and training and fighting as often as I could – trawling the martial arts magazines for weekend tournaments.

Then one day in America planes flew into towers. At the time I did not grasp the antagonism and extremism which had led to this moment, but it seemed to me the call to arms of the age; *of my age*. I very vaguely knew of the Taliban and Afghanistan. They were names mentioned on the television between more interesting programmes. When news of it came over the radio, the man I was working with, a Falklands veteran, nodded like a sage. The world had changed, he said.

It was around that time that the media seemed to assure me that I and all other Westerners had been attacked by brown, Muslim terrorists who liked killing women with rocks. There was no hint of a rationale leading up to the event that I could identify, they just attacked one day. Although I knew very little about these things, and they seemed so far away, they still made me very angry. I thought again about being a soldier, and for the first time it seemed like a truly moral choice rather than just a way out of boredom. But, once again, I put the feeling to one side. I had a girlfriend then and wanted to train and compete in kickboxing. Those things were my whole life at the time. I thought that maybe I would join one day. I was still young.

By twenty-two I had ambition but little sense. I felt the need to be involved in something, to be involved in something bigger than myself. I considered university – a degree in politics or writing – but I had no qualifications. I had moved to Ipswich by that time and for a while I volunteered with the local refugee group. Ipswich was a 'catchment area' for asylum seekers. For the first time I met people from places I'd only heard about on television: Afghanistan, Iraq, Iran, Somalia. I asked these people about their lives and how they came to be there in this small East Anglian town. They asked me about my life and I felt compelled to go out and be involved in the world they talked about, which in all honesty sounded as exciting as it was tough.

I befriended an Albanian Romany kid a little younger than me, and later on his family became my family. They were very fine people and like so many of these newcomers they were hospitable despite having nothing. These displaced people lived under the constant spectre of being interred in one of the refugee detention camps dotted around the country and then deported back to wherever or whatever they were fleeing. I disagreed with this: I wanted to make the world better, but at that age I didn't want to debate at university or become one of the flaky NGO types I occasionally met at the Refugee Council. I wanted to be at the sharp end.

I repeatedly came back to the idea of the military. I would be paid and there would be the 'three meals a day and roof over your head' that every young man needs. I'd have a uniform and I was sure that girls would queue to swoon over me and my soldier friends. Yet, as I considered joining the military, my mother marched with the two million in London to oppose the government and its plans for war on Iraq. We did not discuss the politics of it. I held a dangerous view that a government was some kind of benign, impartial organization that looked after its citizens. I was a chump ready-made for the army, indifferent, apolitical and working class. The Ancient Greeks called anyone politically uninterested an idiot, it is the origin of the word, and back then I was an idiot by those standards. I was sure that if we were prosecuting wars, it was because the government had identified a need. It must be right. The war drums pounded out through the media and a recruiting sergeant made a convincing case. The question of right or wrong never came up.

In 2003, I wandered into an army careers office where the recruiter – a helicopter pilot with embroidered blue wings on his chest – told me all about military life. In the careers office they offered shiny brochures, tea and polished talk, and it looked a lot more interesting than what I was doing at the time. I did a psychometric test – which asked me to turn cogs the right way and that sort of thing – and scored averagely. I selected three jobs from a list: engineers, cavalry and medical corps. I was offered a place in the engineers and given a starting date for basic training. They switched all my options at the last minute and I ended up going in as a logistics specialist. They said that kind of detail was easy to change later. This was a lie. As it turned out it was extremely hard to move jobs and when I saw the officer in charge of changing trades he assured me I would have to linger around training camps for a long time. I'd spent hours outside running, readying myself. In my leaving card from the restaurant I worked at one of my colleagues wrote 'make sure you kill some ragheads'. I told him I would and it still shames me, and I went away to learn war.

Chapter 2

I reached the small Surrey train station in the sunshine to find a horde of other recruits. You can spot them easily, even when you are one of them: we were all jittery, with cropped hair, and trying to butch up. We were led onto a bus and delivered through the gates of Army Training Regiment Pirbright to begin the Common Military Syllabus (Recruits). Rallied by an ancient, shouting corporal, we were marched through the camp to our accommodation. We were out of step and looked ridiculous; we knew nothing about anything here. Then we were fed and issued with a whole number of green and camouflaged items, many of which we never learnt the use for: a confusing mass of camouflage clothing, webbing, pouches, aide-mémoires, straps, respirators (gas masks), chemical warfare suits.

The base itself was spartan, industrial-smelling and every building and fixture seemed worn by either a lack of care or perhaps too much scrubbing, polishing and sweeping – it was hard to tell. Everything was 'bullshit' according to the other recruits, or at least the ones who spoke to us, because there was a hierarchy based on time spent here. The recruits who had been here the longest looked at us with scorn and mocked us. Even to the other recruits we were fresh, and to the instructors we were even lower than that. This camp turned normal people into soldiers bound for different parts of the army: privates for the logistics corps, troopers for Household Cavalry and gunners for the Royal Artillery. But at this stage we were all just called Recruit.

On our first night we were called to the central room of our block for the corporal's amusement. We sat on the floor wide-eyed and nervous – forty new bonehead haircuts and standard issue tracksuits. 'Okay, lads,' the squat corporal told his captives, 'if at any time while you're here anybody tries to bum you, you should take one for the team!' We laughed the laughter of sycophants. 'And remember,' he waggled a finger, 'you're only gay if you push back.'

From then on you had to march everywhere and call people by their ranks – even privates. This reminded us that we were only recruits. I only failed to do this once when I was peering through a window at a squad of recruits marching past the scoff-house (mess hall). Their tiny Scots corporal saw me, halted them perfectly and then ran to confront me. Staring up at me, he raised himself on tiptoes. 'You eyeballin' me, wee man?' he slurred in his near-impenetrable Glaswegian. He was slight, wiry, and glowed alcoholically. 'No, mate,' I assured him, unsure of the penalty for having eyes. His face reddened. 'Mate,' he rasped. When I explained I was in Week One he let it go, satisfied he had beefed himself up to those present. He scuttled off and switched his abuse back to his own charges.

For the first few days the corporals were limited to shouting at us. The regulations said they couldn't damage us until we had passed a medical. Once the medics had checked us over we were fucked about at all times as we stumbled through the fundamentals: boot polishing, uniform ironing and foot drill. Within days we started to bond by ransacking each others' rooms dressed in gas masks, boots and full green, military long johns in the dark hours. We adopted soldierly habits, swearing, fighting and piss-taking, and the weakest were routinely turned upon.

The transformation had begun. But we were still only panicky recruits, our first names trimmed and replaced with numbers. I was now 25193317, Recruit Glenton. We were always alert to the shouts around us and always relieved when it was someone else being ripped into. Our lives and value were measured in weeks served. People would ask each other what week they were in, and this provided a hierarchy. The first serious test was to carry out a set of drill movements as a squad on the parade square. After this you could march yourself to eat bad food, rather the being marched by the corporals. This seemed like a privilege to us.

I was starting to love it, the marching and the shouting and the joking and the new friends. Even the language started to seep into us: fuck this, cunt that, and wanker everything and scrote-bag every fucker. On weekend leave I found this language jarred with the real world. Fuck it, I thought. Who needed the real world? I was going to be a soldier forever. I went back to training eager and feeling like I should have joined earlier and not wasted years in dead-end jobs in kitchens and factories. I was good at this stuff and it was little strain. Just turn up on time, pay the compliments, salute the posh blokes, call the corporals corporal and the sergeants sergeant, charge around the woods, iron your kit, get paid – easy life.

We had been taught to strip our rifles down for cleaning, except sights and a few other parts which were reserved for armourers. This would have been 'illegal stripping'. On the ranges during our shooting test my rear sight had come loose and, as it slid free, I got increasingly inaccurate. We were not allowed to adjust them. I told our sergeant this and he told me I should have adjusted it. In the army, this kind of thing is called 'being seen off'. This means being stitched up and is what happens in the Soldier Box, away from civilian eyes and universal sense. I failed the test, was sent back – 'back-trooped' – by a week to retake the test, and re-assigned to another troop that was a week behind us.

In this new group – Peninsular Troop – we were taught by infantrymen from the Guards and the Green Howards. The guardsmen were cracked: they told us that in the Household Division the word 'yes' did not exist. Instead, they just said 'sarnt' (meaning sergeant) as a matter of etiquette. It is the only approved affirmative in the Guards, they said. In addition, when they entered and left the parade square for drill practice they halted and saluted the concrete expanse; drill was religion to them. One of them told us that when we had our final passing out parade we should aim to be so crisp, so smart and so superb that our very posture and bearing seemed to bellow to the onlookers: 'Look at me. I am chocolate. LICK ME.'

The Green Howard was from the north of England and hated southerners. He would single out a particularly southern-sounding soldier and repeatedly scream 'Dawkins, you are a cunt', into his face in his best cockney accent. He was bitter about having got all the way through SAS selection only to be rejected. His personality hadn't squared with the Special Forces. We felt this was understandable. I later heard he was kicked out of the army, something about punching recruits.

At times we would hear our names bellowed as the NCOs summoned us for a round of abuse. We'd stop what we were doing and scuttle out of our rooms, snap to attention at the door of the central room, and rattle off our names and numbers. 'Ah, recruit so-and-so!' one of them would cackle, 'come in.' They would lounge around the edge of the room as we were interrogated about nothing in particular. 'So, recruit so-and-so,' one corporal would ask as others looked on, 'tell me, have you ever tasted your own semen?' Any laughter from the subject would be met with a demand to know what 'the fuck' was funny. Do you think you're hard? Or funny? Are you a fucking joker? Are you a clown of some kind? 'No corporal' would be the only acceptable reply.

'So Glenton,' I was asked once, 'what is THAT?'

'Corporal?' I asked.

An accusing finger shot up to point at a mole under my eye. 'THAT. Is it a fucking Coco Pop?'

This was accompanied by a new round of chortles.

'Yes, corporal, it's a Coco Pop,' I confirmed.

'Well be more fucking careful at breakfast then, Recruit Glenton.'

We soon moved on to weapons training, field craft, more drill, tabbing (marching or running with a backpack) and lots of time in the gym wearing ridiculous blue short-shorts. As some kind of encouragement our corporals would egg us on: 'You'll fucking run when you've got twenty hairy-arsed Iraqis chasing you.'

The corporals were often angry – our stupidity was painful to them. One day on the firing ranges, as we lay with our elbows crunching in the damp gravel, firing rounds at the targets, one of our number managed to upset an instructor, a mouthy southern corporal. We all froze as he rounded on the recruit, who had shot an angry look at an NCO. 'If you ever fucking look at him like that again, chicken lips, I'll fucking shoot you myself!' He checked himself as we all looked on. 'Don't tell anyone I said that,' he added. We all shifted our gaze, straight down the range for the rest of the day. Staring down the lengths of our rifles we revised in our minds whether chickens had lips.

We were up early and late to bed. I found the fatigue manageable after the initial shock and was determined to pass through with minimal fuss. Some people left after a few weeks, citing a change of heart and I thought them foolish. I reasoned that this period did not represent the army per se; it was a rushed, half-cocked introduction. I kept my head down, blending in as much as I could; the last thing I wanted was notoriety. I was once even pulled up for my obscurity in a report. A Scots corporal – one known to lift his kilt during drill practice to expose what he termed the tartan torpedo – told me I needed to look like I was struggling more, otherwise I wasn't trying. I told him I would struggle as much as I could. I felt at all times like a fellow traveller – other people moaned and griped and I pushed on. There was no way that this would beat me, it wasn't even the proper army yet.

We were taken on a battlefield tour of Belgium and France. We saw graveyards of grim, dark stones for the Germans and white crosses for our lot. Here and there we stopped and looked at surviving fortifications that seemed to spring weirdly out of rolling green farmland. We visited the Menin Gate – a monolithic war memorial – where a select few were allowed to lay a wreath at the service while the rest of us looked on and tried to feel morbid. The occasion was treated very seriously and seemed to demand seriousness. Our instructors told us we should think deeply about this because some of us would die soon in the wars. I thought deeply about this and quietly dismissed the idea that it would be any of us getting killed. I do not know if any of my friends from training died, except one of our sergeants who was okay to us and stole our fags a lot. 'If you're smoking,' he would say in his Sunderland accent, 'then sergeant is smoking.' An IED killed him in Afghanistan. He was a guardsman and only thirty years old.

After the first weeks of training and the battlefield tour we began to spend more and more time out in the training area, learning to survive the cold and lack of sleep, and doing what one of our instructors termed 'aggressive camping'. I liked being there, even though it was uncomfortable and the exercises were very basic. It felt good. To start with we would tab out and then form a 'harbour' area, a circle of outwards facing pits in which we lived and pretended to die when attacked. We would then do patrols and reconnaissance, and at night we would get attacked. If we lived we would bug out (retreat) in the dark.

Our troop commander, a lieutenant from the Grenadier Guards, schooled us in what to do when attacked. He carried himself like a man whose ancestors had commanded common scum like us at Waterloo. 'When one is ambushed in the harbour area,' he told us, 'one must get out of one's scratcher (sleeping bag) and pack one's bergen (backpack) aggressively.' When attacked we packed our bags violently and mock-fought our way out, running into trees and each other. Afterwards the instructors would bring us back and we would look for all the things we'd left behind: sleeping bags, mess-tins, rifles, boots, other recruits and packets of sweets. A 'beasting' (hard exercise) followed and Willy the Whistle became our master. We'd have to crawl a muddy circuit on our bellies on one blast, run on two blasts and do press-ups in the mud on three – all with the stated aim of making our eyes bleed.

The officer took us out to learn how to do a reconnaissance patrol, a particular type of manoeuvre which we were told involved the maximum of stealth and field craft. 'So are we going to sneak around, sir?' I asked him. He scoffed disparagingly, 'The British Army does not simply... *sneak around*.'

None of this felt particularly real. In fact it felt like we were doing most of our exercises on a rubbish tip. The landscape was strewn with empty ration packs which soldiers were meant to bury after use. Animals dug these up so all our training areas were covered in plastic and the debris of pretend warfare. Another hazard was left over from years of shovel reconnaissance, where a man, his rifle and a shovel travel out into the bushes to shit. Her Majesty's restricted woodlands of Britain are mined with shit and plastic. This tactical activity – once known as 'Squat, Squeeze and Cover' – was now frowned upon and Portaloos had been scattered around the woods where soldiers would go for their tactical field shits. We were told to patrol in groups, or at least pairs, to these brightly coloured shrines in a proper soldierly fashion.

Once *in situ*, you peer into the woods over the sights of your weapon to protect your comrade while he squeezes inside the toilet with his webbing, rifle and helmet. You then switch. This is preparation for the war. We were told they have portable shitters in Iraq and Afghanistan as well. Portaloos, I figured, are omens of freedom and democracy in the sand and are rated among our greatest weapons in the War on Terror.

Training continued to be good fun. We were forming bonds with each other, except for a few 'gobshites' and 'jack' (selfish) bastards. When our fights broke out the instructors would stop them but they were not overly concerned. After all, we were learning how to survive, fight and kill – albeit in a rudimentary way. We were only destined for the corps, not the infantry. They're the ones who do the real killing. Rudimentary killing was our game. We would not be considered fully trained until we had been at our units for six months. But, as the instructors told us, if you kept your mouth shut, turned up on time and looked like you were struggling you would get through it.

Our lives were punctuated with 'show parades', a punishment for such sins as inadequate ironing. You had to give a bold, clear announcement for the inspecting officer: 'Sir,

25193317 Recruit Glenton, Peninsular Troop, 105 Squadron RLC, week eight showing combat trousers properly ironed, sir.' During one of these punishments the scruffiest officer I had ever seen emerged from the guardroom. He was an outrageous toff with hair down his back and a stupid accent down pat. His uniform was in what we called shit-state and a swollen black Lab wheezed at his feet. All he needed was a Barbour jacket and a shotgun. He looked us up and down paying no attention, and then orated, 'Clearly, it's imperative on operations around the world, in places like Irarrrk, B'zzniaar and Arfgarnistaarrn, that we need smart, well-turned out soldiers. I do not wish to see you here again.' He swaggered off and left us wondering where we'd plug in the iron in the desert. The duty sergeant met our gazes, and shrugged. 'What a cock,' the sergeant said. Senior NCOs alone do not fear officers, unless they have maps in their hands and want to navigate.

Every soldier in every army has stories from training, all rooted in the same themes – screaming corporals, early mornings, and inspections with unattainable standards, bullshit and violence. It was here we were lectured in the 'Values of the Army' by the padre: Courage, Discipline and Respect for Others, Integrity, Loyalty and Selfless Commitment. It is strange now to have learned about ethics in the army and from a priest of all people. Apparently, this is what priests are meant to do. Having been raised beyond God's earshot, I had no idea they were other than decorative. Iraq and Afghanistan, I would find, were conflicts that required moral vaccination.

There were also informal lessons on what we were being trained for. We endured nuclear-biological-chemical warfare lessons – during which we were CS-gassed while the instructors filmed our trailing, gas-induced snot and misery. We were also taught that when a nuclear blast wave comes it is called a positive wave. This name is deceptive – it does not mean the wave is essentially good. Because of this essential un-goodness we are to lie down. When it returns we should still be prone – this wave is called the negative wave. We lie down so that we may continue to fight after the nuclear detonation. Presumably, our fight would be with whoever else had known to lie down and over whatever is left to fight for after a nuclear blast. After this lesson we were assembled and told by an instructor that whatever our job, our goal was to 'kill cunts', or to get others into a position where they could 'kill cunts'. We were all about cunt-killing.

This disparity between the padre's line and the one we were to apply was clear. After our Values and Standards lessons, once we were marched out of the padre's proximity, we would be told, 'Don't listen to that soppy old fucker. Just do what you are told, that's all you worry about. Thinking is out of your pay scale.' Soldiers do not work with the padre. He is normally trying to get people to talk to him and stop hiding when they see him coming. Soldiers, however, are rarely out of sight of NCOs. We took our cues on ethics from the NCOs, who would beast us and occasionally threaten to shoot us, not the priests.

At the end of our training, when we had passed all of our basic tests in shooting, marching, obeying and being abused, we had a passing out parade – a ceremony where we marched around the parade square in front of our families before being inspected by a senior officer. We carried out some overly elaborate drill moves as a full troop of thirty or so soldiers. We managed to fluff most of it and after we'd finished a visiting colonel strutted our three ranks inspecting, fawning and talking rubbish to us. I was unmoved. I had no family there to see my shiny toecaps and no. 2 dress (formal dress). It was my own day. I was going to be a soldier now and felt like I was part of something good and wholesome.

The logistics soldiers were sent down the road from Pirbright to Deepcut in order to learn to steer ourselves and others towards or away from violence, depending on the situation we would be facing. We were still treated like children, but called private instead of recruit. Many of our families were more concerned about a son posted here than to Iraq. Deepcut was a grim old training camp – home of the School of Logistics – and had a sinister reputation. By this time pickaxe handles had been swapped back to rifles for the guard shift, as a number of recruits had managed to shoot themselves in the head multiple times. A huge legal battle had ensued with much squirming from the Ministry of Defence and Army. We never pressed the topic.

At Deepcut you stayed quiet and tried to get through your course as quickly as possible. After my trade training I was put into a driving course. This consisted of a week or so of intensive lessons and then test after test until we either passed or were made to be chefs – chefs did not need to have a vehicle licence. We were constantly threatened with being forced to become an army chef – no one there wanted to be an egg-flipper or a cabbage technician. I did six driving tests and barely managed to escape.

I was despatched with three other soldiers on an otherwise empty coach to the military driving school to do our truck licence. We sat in the hangars of the old airbase for days at a time waiting for someone to pass their test so we could take their position. When this was finally done I returned to Deepcut and did two weeks of guard, standing on the gate in all weathers as people came and went. We stopped and searched random cars to punctuate the boredom. I had asked to be posted to Colchester, which was approved. I was despatched for some pre-posting leave with papers telling me not to be late to my unit.

Chapter 3

We were told to choose the three regiments we most wanted for our first posting and I got my first choice: 13 Air Assault Support Regiment. Based in Colchester, it had a good boxing team and looked more interesting than the standard logistics units in that we got maroon berets and bigger badges and it was said to be more *warlike*. Its soldiers were trained to move things – people, fuel, water, ammunition – wherever they needed to go. The regiment had a fleet of vehicles and the specialisms within the regiment ranged from drivers and logistics specialists to petroleum operators who specialized in the transport and storage of fuels.

We provided this logistical support to the airborne brigade and the paratroopers who hated us for being 'crap-hats' (non-paras). Nonetheless we got to wear maroon berets like them. The paras – while professionally aggressive – were unlikely to be parachuted en masse into anything ever again. The epoch of mass parachute assaults had ended but it still looked good to have paratroopers. I disliked heights but planned to take the course – it meant more money.

I walked through the gates one morning and was quickly processed and told I would be in 82 Squadron. I was put into a room with three others. A St Lucian, a Scottish kid named MacDougal, and Dobbin who was a shit-magnet (a soldier who attracts trouble) I knew from Deepcut. I never knew anyone who messed up so much, or got shouted at so often. We thought perhaps his mother had made him join. These kinds of kids go one of two ways: they are either abandoned as a liability or kept on as a kind of dopey mascot. We tried our best to look after him. MacDougal was the scruffiest soldier I had ever met. Once, when he turned up on parade in clip (a scruffy state) he was told he would have looked scruffy naked. Despite this he was a regular Casanova and very successful with women. I started drinking with him to pick up stragglers and it turned out he was also good company.

Dobbin was terribly unfit and always late. He constantly exasperated our administrative sergeant, Nasty Bob, who was a professionally unpleasant senior NCO. He was also commando and airborne trained, very fit and completely tapped. I suspect he saw in Dobbin a younger version of himself and he tried to shape him. He took him on runs and beasted him and tried to stop him chain-smoking, eating kebabs every night and drinking litres of Coke. These long, arduous runs were called Bobercise. I imagine every army in the world has a Bob and a Dobbin. The sound of Nasty Bob shouting in frustration at Dobbin as he messed up simple tasks was the elevator music of our working day.

The tension in a working unit was different to that in basic training. Any new private who believed that passing training would elevate them was soon crushed. You were a nig (new in green) or a crow (new bloke), and the last batch of nigs had been waiting for the next batch so as to assume the role of slightly-less new bloke in order to be able to avoid shit tasks and duties. I had picked up enough cant and bearing so that people assumed this was a second posting. At twenty-two I was geriatric by these standards and as soon as I arrived I came nose to nose with my sergeant major. He took exception to my not standing rigidly to attention as soon as he appeared – albeit unidentifiable in civilian clothing. From then on I realized that bullshit was maintained here and wheeled out on occasion. This was my first clash with the hierarchy and my only clash for years. After that I built a rapport with the seniors, mostly by just turning up on time and not moaning when I did get assigned a shit job.

One morning after I'd been in the field army a week or so – the camp was woken by the regimental sergeant major setting off all the fire alarms. It was around 0500 hours. He had gathered his senior NCOs from the sergeant's mess and they screamed at us until we were all on parade. Some of us were in no. 2 dress, others in sheets and some in boxer shorts or half of a uniform. He paced the great square as we gathered and waited, tapping his stick on the tarmac. 'Somebody,' he roared in his Northern Irish accent, 'was outside my regimental HQ early this morning, smashing up the garden furniture that my HQ staff sit on.' There was silence and hundreds of sidelong glances. 'You will all go from here, and reassemble in ten minutes in full no. 2 dress.' He went on, still pacing, 'After that you will parade again in combat order.' He let it sink in. The RSM timed threats expertly. 'This will continue until I have a confession.' He faced us squarely, putting both hands on his stick and leaning on it. The sun was coming up by then. 'Begin'.

We did about three changes before someone grassed up the guilty soldiers. The two offenders, a pair of Geordie lance-jacks (lance-corporals), were marched away for discipline. It turned out they had staggered into camp after a night on the beer and seen the plastic garden furniture on the grass by RHQ. They had been smashing it up in the balmy night when the RSM returned from a conference. He had driven back overnight and pulled up as they were throwing chairs at the building. They had run off before the RSM could identify them.

The level of prejudice surprised me and took some of the gleam off my shiny new world. At times it was worse in the army than outside, perhaps because prejudices were institutionalized. We had Fijians, Nepalese, black and white Africans, Scotsmen and Ulstermen and a gay chef. He was constantly sniped at for his orientation and he sniped back admirably. Contrary to recent PR exercises, gays are not generally appreciated in the British Army.

The white NCOs opined openly that the African soldiers were not only lazy and disrespectful but also – and worst of all – black. The NCOs would assign punishments accordingly and the Africans would complain. This would start the 'race card' debate. This saw strenuous denials from the racists and they would fall back pathetically on a standard excuse: length of service. 'I've been in the army ten, fifteen, eighteen years. I'm not a racist!'

Bizarrely, this fallacy often worked. Length of service seemed to impart a special voodoo-like force field against all accusations in the military. I saw this time and time again. These characters would then switch back to their racist rants when the Africans were out of earshot: 'Shouldn't be in the army, lazy fucking niggers, fucking skiving again.' The spiel we were given in basic training about there being 'no black, yellow, brown or white' in the army, 'only green', didn't seem to exist outside basic training, though occasionally the term 'fucking non-swimmers' was substituted for 'fucking niggers'; most of the Africans and Caribbeans could not swim and on their personnel documents non-swimmers was the term used. I wasn't going to join in, so I kept my head down and learned quite quickly that when anyone starts a sentence with 'I'm not a racist, but… ', they are a racist.

Likewise, women were a sore point, routinely treated as what the army terms 'ginger cousins' rather like the Royal Air Force. They generally couldn't carry as much, had periods, cried, and didn't put out when required. They also smelled far too nice – which was distracting – and they made the camp look untidy. They nonetheless were expected to adapt to the maleness of the culture: spitting, swearing and fighting were the criteria and many contributed admirably.

The physical culture was punishing but I embraced it. We did at least three training sessions a week and were encouraged to do more – these were beastings designed to push people physically and break them if possible. Every Friday we assembled for commanding officers' physical training. This was normally a run in boots or a speed march with weight on our backs.

Physical training instructors (PTIs) are the prima donnas of any regiment and a gathering of them looks like a second-tier boy band. These mythical creatures can normally be found in the gym doing lunges, wearing crisp white short-shorts and permanent tans and their hair was often worn longer than regulation and crafted delicately and carefully. I often wondered if they got up especially early and styled each other. That summer we regularly ran a circuit through the woods in blazing heat, often in boots, sometimes carrying weight or even each other up hills, through rivers and so on. Once, during a fireman's carry that seemed to go for miles, a corporal shat himself. The PTI applauded him and told the rest of us that this was exactly the kind of effort he wanted to see. We should count ourselves lucky to be going to war with men committed enough to shit themselves with effort before giving up. During another beasting, when the regiment gathered for a water break, the 'elite' 63 Squadron was missing. They were hiding in the woods. 'Skive to survive' was our adage on commanding officers' physical training, which was fine unless you got caught taking it easy at the back. We were all thrashed in the heat for the sins of these few with many press-ups and sprints and fireman's carries.

I loved the soldiering life. That system is designed to create a robust character and it made me robust physically and mentally. The military also teaches you that it's socially acceptable to explode. Colchester has been a military town since the Romans and perhaps for this reason the inhabitants were adept at spotting soldiers and all but the least scrupulous of its womenfolk avoided us. We would regularly go to one of the two clubs or the various bars and pubs, and then batter each other or some unfortunate before devouring a kebab. Midweek, if we'd failed to 'trap' a woman – which was often, given we were a charmless herd of drunk soldiers – we would stumble back across camp to our rooms giving each other drunken abuse every step of the way. Sometimes we had grazed knuckles, split lips or aching mandibles and we stunk of kebabs and beer.

Such was the lifestyle of a junior private or crow. We had no rank to lose. We were closeted in the army and we were fit, strong and aggressive young soldiers. We would drink all night and sweat it out on a morning run. Violence was fine, even encouraged, and certainly expected. However, if you got caught or arrested then you discovered how much the sergeant major hated the paperwork and you would suffer doubly from the punishment and his attentions.

Getting on a sporting team was the way forward, we were told. Some people get into a sport and never go on tour but still fly up the ranks. I joined the boxing team and we trained all day long for weeks. It was immense. We were permanently in sports kit and went running at dawn and hit bags and pads and each other for three hours a day. The squadron boxing event was approaching and we threw ourselves into it. The medicals came around and I was barred from entering. I couldn't believe it. I had been kickboxing for years by then and never even had a medical. I'd been punched and kicked in the grid (face) more times than I could recall, with no ill effect. Apparently my eyes were sub-standard. I was told to get into uniform and report back to my troop.

I went with the regiment to a training area in Norfolk, down on the whole thing until I realized what we were doing. We were to 'play the enemy' for a battalion of paratroopers who were going to Iraq. We were given vehicles and drove around wearing Middle Eastern scarves for a week, playing cowboys and Indians – or rather, soldiers and insurgents. We finished the week off by rioting in a village built specifically for training FIBUA (fighting in built up areas). We came in our hoodies and boots, some of us with newspapers stuffed in our clothes knowing we'd be getting a beating. We fought with the lines of paratroopers all day. They were fortified like ancient warriors behind their wall of shields, visors down, and armed with lengths of piping instead of heavy wooden batons. We threw spent baton rounds instead of bricks and got repeatedly beaten up and mock-arrested. It was even better than boxing.

One of our lance corporals managed to take down the CO of 2 Para (the 2nd Batallion, the Parachute Regiment) with a baton round. The man was prancing behind the line of his men when our boy saw him and chucked the round. It was a good shot. It split his eyebrow open beautifully and all us proxy rioters cheered as he folded and the 2 Para sergeant major dragged him away for treatment. During a break in the rioting he approached us as we sat around. We gawped at his patched-up face and the bloody dressing and he thanked us for our viciousness and told us that we needed to be as cruel as possible as these men were going to Iraq soon, where some of them would likely kill and perhaps die, and they would need to be tough and vicious to survive.

Between bouts we would sit in a barn with a group of Iraqi interpreters who stoked up a huge shisha. These Iraqi expats hired by the army for realism were great. They called everyone sarge and when we were rioting they would bang drums, dance and start chants, which we would mimic: 'Down, down Bush,' we sang to their cues, 'Down, down Blair, down, down Ah-mer-ica!' We fought with the paras all day until we were mottled with bruises and cuts and we could hardly lift our arms to block their blows.

I, along with two other privates, managed to make a baby paratrooper cry as we played at rioting. The paras were strung out in a line between buildings and this lone crow was between a building and a fence. The others couldn't reach us with the plastic pipes they swung in lieu of batons. Some of these weapons rattled because the paratroopers filled them with stones and sealed the ends with tape to bite us harder and bloody us better. The kid had a bigger shield than the others. We asked him why – was he fucking new or something? We bullied him until he blubbered and started lashing out with his baton. One of the exercise marshals in his high-visibility vest eventually pulled him out of the game.

The final exercise had us huddling in buildings all night, loading hundreds of magazines with blanks. As dawn broke we squatted in the streets like guerrillas, faces covered with bandannas and keffiyehs. Through the mist the paras came in vehicles and on foot. We blasted off hundreds of blanks on automatic, and threw dozens of smoke grenades. The paras screamed as they followed us into the buildings and through the rat-holes which connected them. Anyone they caught was beaten for good measure. The rest escaped. Then suddenly the exercise was stopped by the marshals. One of the top-heavy Land Rovers had rolled on a corner. One paratrooper had broken his arm, another got his helmeted head wedged between the roll cage and the concrete and an unfortunate Iraqi interpreter was taken away in an ambulance. The need for realism in training often led to casualties before anyone ever got to a war zone.

We played the enemy in a lot of exercises. It seemed to be our role and was much better than sitting in camp. We were dressed as Chechen-type rebels and given old Kalashnikovs brought back from war and deactivated for training. We wandered around the Brecon Beacons in Wales so the Pathfinder selection (reconnaissance) course could observe us from the hills and log our activities. These guys were some of the toughest in the brigade and had a fearsome reputation. Some of our lads got bored as we hid in an old farm. One of them had brought a football which they covered in fluid from a Cyalume (glow stick) and kicked it around the fields all night. The glow-in-the-dark football crowd later left our machine-gun out on a guard post. The Pathfinders crept in that night and nicked it. The course instructor had gotten sick of our antics and disassembled the gun into its three main parts. He handed each of the troublemakers a piece and pointed to a stone pillar on a hillside a mile or so away. They were made to run over fences, through ditches and bogs to the distant pillar and back until they could go no further. The rest of us held in our laughter. Being an insurgent is all about discipline, the Pathfinders assured us.

We eventually ambushed the would-be Pathfinders in the closing stages and beat them to the ground as ordered, piling on top of them while two of our number – a German speaker and a Ghanaian – ranted at them in foreign languages. We put bags over their heads, plastic-cuffed them and marched them up a hill to a little sheep shed, in which a fizzing radio provided disorienting white noise for our captives.

Back in camp there were whispers of an operational tour coming up and the old hands told us about invading Iraq – the oldest of them had been in both Gulf wars. They told us about machete wounds in Sierra Leone and Kenyan or Belizean or German or Russian and Balkan whores and fly-covered bodies on Rwandan roadsides under a toothless UN mandate and the heat in Iraq and the cold in Bosnia. These veterans told us about waiting near the border to invade Iraq and how the WMD sirens would wail several times per day so they'd have to get into their awful, sweltering chemical warfare suits and respirators and sit in the heat waiting to die, and how the WMD never came because there were no WMD and it had been known that there were none. All those awful, sweating, panting hours had been for nothing and that had pissed them off.

One of the corporals told us that he got D&V (diarrhoea and vomiting) in Iraq and that when you are shitting and puking uncontrollably you just sit in your filth and ask yourself what the fucking point is. A guy from a different squadron told us that he had avoided D&V by simply drinking Coke instead of water for the whole tour and how he had been ordered – straight out of training and eighteen years old – to invade Iraq in a great, lumbering forklift truck with a can of warm Coke in one hand, a single magazine with only twenty rounds in it and a big flashing light on top of the cab which could be seen for miles. Why, he had asked, was that light there winking, marking him out like a bull's-eye? And they had told him the light had to be there for health and safety reasons.

Nasty Bob in particular told a lot of war stories and made them as gory as he could and we were sure they were mostly bullshit but we wanted them to be true. We crows wanted to shit ourselves uncontrollably in the desert then get home and laugh it off. We wanted to bang whores at Rosa's brothel in Belize City and invade countries in inappropriate vehicles and with a lack of ammunition and see bodies covered in flies. We wanted stories to regale birds with and to tell in the pub to our civilian mates who would never get them. They just wouldn't and couldn't know, but we would know and we would be wise, grim-faced and powerful for knowing these war things. I wanted to be in their club and all I had to do now was go to war.

The experienced blokes assured us of blood and gore and plunder and trophies and raw experience we would share with our mates, and we embraced it all. We wanted our own stories and adventures and they wanted us to want them. Then the whispers turned into stronger rumours that we were bound for Afghanistan. By then we were aching for it. The old hands in the regiment would tell us that 'this one's going to be different, not like Iraq'. And they spurred on our yearning with lines that, for the most part, would turn out to be true: '*People treat you differently when you've done a tour… You'll get to do your proper job… There's less bullshit on tour… 13 badly needs a tour… You'll come back rich from tour… You can get loads of cheap shit on tour… Fuck, I need a tour, my wife's pissing me off… People get promoted off the back of tours… I've knocked up some tart, I need a tour… I'm getting done for assault, I bit some civvy cunt's ear off, and so can I come on tour, sir?*'

We started training months before we deployed and we shifted from playing at insurgents to playing at soldiers. The regiment hadn't been on tour since the invasion of Iraq in 2003. By 2005, Afghanistan had reappeared in the media and we were to be among the first into the south of that country. There was much anticipation but in the end we went through a vague series of training activities and started to shoot more often, we practised live-firing vehicle anti-ambush drills, the highlight of which was when one of our Fijians nearly cut our hated sergeant major in two with a GPMG (general purpose machine-gun) as the man ran around manically shouting during live-firing. We practised cordoning and rudimentary mine-probing, vehicle recognition (presumably in case the Taliban started driving tanks or flying Apache helicopters) and other military skills. We were never given firm reasons why we were going or a specific mission to be carried out. We hardly noticed any of that because we were going to a war. I drew from the media and from what little we were told that we'd be ensuring the streets of Britain would be safer because security over there equalled security here. Peace needed to be kept or built from scratch, women needed to be liberated, or maybe everyone needed to be liberated, opium production needed to be stopped. We needed all of these, some of these, many combinations of these.

Chapter 4

About fifty of us were to deploy early as part of the 'pre-pre-advanced party'. The day before our deployment, we were brought to the mess hall of our camp where we queued to be processed by the regimental clerks. We were given dog tags and Ministry of Defence wills to fill out as we sat and waited. When it was all done, I was assigned to the baggage party. Myself and another private left in the early hours of the next morning in a truck stacked with bags and equipment and we drove through the night to RAF Lyneham. Once there, we humped the bags onto a big steel weighing plate built into a hangar floor. Bleary-eyed airmen tallied the weight and signed it off. We milled about until the rest of our squadron arrived.

We were sent into the departure lounge as it filled with more soldiers and a company of Royal Marines. We boarded by rank, beginning with the most senior. It was my first time on a plane and I was flying to war. We were instructed to keep our body armour and helmets with us. Filing across the tarmac, we boarded an RAF TriStar passenger plane where I sat next to two marines. Even to me they seemed young – even more childlike as they munched on packets of sweets.

We stopped in Dubai and were herded into a fenced enclosure next to the runway, to wait in segregation and smoke as many cigarettes as we could while our plane was refuelled. I imagined that British soldiers in uniform were not popular in Middle Eastern airport lounges. We got back on and flew towards Kabul.

The sun came up and I saw Central Asia from the air. It seemed barren and brown, with occasional spidery tracks and snow-capped peaks. It looked like the legendary Hindu Kush, though in truth I had no idea where we were. I vaguely knew that we didn't like Iran, so assuming we had to avoid its airspace, we were perhaps over Pakistan or Turkmenistan. Over the tannoy we were ordered to don body armour and helmets as we descended into Kabul. I was afraid and excited and out of the window I could see this was a spectacular and rugged place. The runway was flanked to its edge by sheer rock capped in white. We bumped down into Afghanistan and taxied. We disembarked and trudged the tarmac amongst the marines. It was icy cold and fresh. I'd expected heat but it was early morning. We were immediately processed into theatre by RAF movement controllers before being herded onto a Hercules amid piles of kit secured under cargo nets, and we took off heading south.

Kandahar was choking with dust and full of Americans. The temperatures would reach the mid-fifties that summer. A bus took us to our living area and we sifted through baggage to find our own. We settled into the eight-man tents that the Royal Engineers had put up. There wasn't much to do in the first few weeks, so we waited and acclimatized. We got our bush hats tailored from the massive brim they came with to the little one which army fashion required. If just the very tip of your nose got sunburnt you knew you were trendy.

Kandahar Airfield (KAF) was a big, American-run facility where most of us would be based for the duration of the tour. The desert shimmered and yet there was some kind of stillness to it. Every movement seemed to catch the eye and anything darker than light dun stood out powerfully. There was one afternoon when rain spat down at us, mottling the dust. For the next seven months our only water came from showers, taps and the pallets of bottled mineral water which were dotted all over the place. Mineral water companies were making a killing out of the war.

Kandahar Airfield was like an American town and though there were soldiers from many nations here the Americans were the most visible because they were loud and wore ridiculous aviator sunglasses and drove up-armoured Humvees with skulls stencilled on the doors. I saw a particularly amazing American one day: he stomped bowlegged like a cowboy with a pistol on his hip, the blue-grey digitized combats they wear and a black Stetson-type hat with clean gold braid like General Custer. Our own blokes, the ones who had been in Iraq, rolled their eyes having seen his type before. Apaches and Chinooks circled constantly, night and day, and Harriers roared up the runway regularly as they went on ops.

We ate in the US DFAC (dining facility). We heard the Americans got forty dollars a day per man for food against our few pounds. We knew our eating with them wouldn't last. You could tell it was too good to be true. They had a vast array of food and facilities and ate lobster twice a week, while outside the wire Afghanistan burned. Here I got an impression of the amount of money that the US was pumping into Afghanistan, albeit only to keep its cannon-fodder in gumbo, burgers and Mountain Dew. There was a boardwalk being built and already on it were a Burger King and a Pizza Hut. I avoided these places, but some of the others didn't and went down with food poisoning. We knew then we were at McWar.

At the start of the tour we were based in the logistics park where local contractors were laying the concrete for the k-spans (huge corrugated hangars). We only had a couple of tents then and as we worked, more and more shipping containers appeared on 'jingly' trucks painted with bright, exotic murals and so named because of the skirts of dangling, clinking chains. All the way from Karachi the trucks came, containers often tied onto them with rope. The chains and decorations were said to keep the devils away. The containers were lifted off by the RTCH (rough terrain container handler), a massive vehicle with tyres eight to ten feet high designed to lift shipping containers. Its mechanical arm lifted them off, stacking the containers three high around the logistics park. The native drivers were incredibly capable. A common sight would be a truck with a twenty-foot flatbed carrying a forty-foot container.

One of my first duties was guarding the 'chogies' (derogatory term for locals) as they built our Portaloos. A corporal from my squadron and I were put in charge of guarding them and dishing out bottles of water as they clipped the toilets together. The corporal was severely pissed off at this demeaning task the whole day and it amused me that he felt hard done by but, once again, Portaloos are the bastions of Western civilization and had to be guarded by us and our rifles.

The only officer who had deployed with us was our squadron 2IC (second in command), a small, blonde woman who had developed a vicious cold sore on her lip. It got worse over the tour as she scratched at the untreated wound. She would gather us together every day like a squawking prefect and demand daily reports. One of our number was an indifferent commando – irreverent and sarcastic to officers and anyone who wasn't commando-trained as a matter of principle. Out of boredom in the first few weeks he had taken to playing a game where he would relate a fictional catastrophe in which only my own section commander died. 'Imagine,' he would say, 'we were overrun by Nazis, or a mortar landed right here next to us, but only he died.' This went on through many versions all of which described the death of my corporal, until our own leader stopped talking to him. After that the commando would steal his notebook and hide it until he threw a tantrum. 'What have you achieved today, corporal?' the 2IC demanded of the commando, clearly thinking in terms of the war effort. He paused, drawing slowly on a cigarette, then pulled off his hat and held it up, 'I got my hat tailored, ma'am.'

The three different troops – material, combat supply, and brigade logistics – set up in tents on the log park. The tents were flimsy, but we had experienced soldiers with us who made us fill sandbags to weigh down the edges of our tent. They laughed when the sandstorm came like a wall of dust that seemed to stretch miles high. It blew out of the desert and I thought I felt raindrops before it hit, but I cannot be sure. The Fijians warned me to get under cover. They had seen many storms in Iraq. But I had wrapped my scarf around my mouth and wanted to stand in it. I pulled down my issue goggles as it hit, and the grit scratched at my skin. The other troops' tents collapsed in moments and my troop mocked them. We were jack (unhelpful) from the lowest man to the troop commander. The storm passed and it was the only one we saw.

Ammo troop, which was five or six of us, worked out of the ammunition site which was on the far side of the airfield, out past the circular shit-pit where sewage was processed and where a mannequin dressed in combat uniform sat in a folding chair next to the pit, holding a fishing rod extending out over the surface. Every day that we drove out to the ammo site, we passed the Romanian contingent who lived opposite the pit of shit. These soldiers were mistaken for Russians at first, by both the locals and us. They carried battered Kalashnikovs and drove huge soviet-style APCs (armoured personnel carriers) that looked like wheeled steel coffins. They wore permanent scowls, perhaps, due to their proximity to the shit-pit. The Romanians spent much of their time on guard in the towers which dotted the perimeter. These were made out of stacked shipping containers with sections cut out of the sides. Their rules of engagement – we were told – were loose, meaning that they shot pretty much anything that wandered too close to the perimeter, be it cows, dogs or anything else.

The ammo site itself was along a gravelled track and we were told to stick to it as the verges had not yet been de-mined. We drove along one end of the airfield – sometimes as Harrier jets roared metres overhead to take off – and then along one side of the runway. Halfway along we turned off through a kind of scrapyard vehicle park with mounds of baked earth piled here and there, through the pitted blast area that was used by the EOD (explosive ordnance disposal) troops to detonate unexploded bombs and mines and then down a long, exposed track that wound towards the ammo site. There were ditches on each side of the track and low fences decorated with mine tape. Here, several times a week, we would see local de-miners sweating in their armour and visors as they probed and scratched carefully in the earth for exploding devices. They would work their way across the ground under the guidance of a Western adviser who observed them from one of the ubiquitous folding chairs, a safe distance behind. The ammo site, with its high fences all around, had been set up out here so the military base would survive if it all blew up. It was also in the middle of a minefield someone had sewn years back – maybe the Soviets, maybe someone else.

The site itself was large, maybe a kilometre long and two thirds as wide. Just inside the wire there was another deep ditch and then a perimeter track. Gravel tracks criss-crossed the site linking the ESHs (explosive storehouses), which were still being built. The foundations had been cleared and the wide layers of honeycombed canvas were being filled with soil to form the blast walls for the storehouses. At the gate of the ammo site was a tent with two Canadian infantrymen and a jeep. The lean, brown soldiers fresh from operations would rotate every twenty-four hours. This was an easy time for them. The on-site Canadian ammunition technician was an enormously fat man – a corporal from Newfoundland who had a fridge in his trailer stacked with snacks and soft drinks. He was socially needy and quite literally like the fat kid at school and was glad whenever he had company. He would ride around on his quad-bike and rush over to see us when we arrived, panting heavily. He was killing time until he could go home. He told us that when he got back to Canada he was being posted to a submarine base to pamper nukes.

We took over the site from a bored Royal Engineer who'd looked after the ammunition for six months. He had two or three containers for the small arms ammunition and that was his main concern. He popped open a container and showed us a modern weapon of war: a suicide vest wrapped in plastic. It had failed to function and been stripped off the would-be dead man. The vest was meticulously well made, but had ripped in one or two places where coins, meant to serve as shrapnel, spilled out of it inside the plastic wrapping. They were American coins. The irony was brutal. It was going to be sent back to the UK for exploitation – to be examined by boffins and used to build our knowledge of suicide tactics.

Until the ESHs were ready, the rest of the UK ammunition – explosives and missiles and grenades – was stored between two long berms at that time. Berms are long mounds of earth usually ploughed up to hinder tanks or as a kind of fortification. These two were close together and a long pit was further excavated in the centre. They were like two funeral barrows around a hundred and fifty metres long. Instead of a boat bound for Valhalla, the centre of it was lined with more shipping containers, each stacked with different types of bangs and bombs. A Canadian berm ran parallel to ours. Our berm was our workplace while the storehouses were built. This area was flat, and through the haze and heat we could see Three Mile Hill – a long, high rocky feature over which the Chinooks and their Apache escorts would disappear and later return.

Our Fijian lance corporal pulled a rusty, dirt-encrusted sword out of our berm one day. I am no archaeologist, but from the look of this sword I imagined it had been there a long time and had survived the bulldozer intact. We stuck the blade into the earth of the berm where we had put up our little tent and it went missing a week later. I kick myself when I think about it now – it was a rare, beautiful and storied thing. Personally, I think the Canadians plundered it. What I did know then was that swords are for fighting and soldiers don't give up their arms carelessly. The idea of ancient soldiers preceding us appealed to me and I wondered about the man who'd lost his sword. Could it have been from the time of Alexander, the man who gave his name to Kandahar centuries ago, on his way to smooch Roxanne.

Early in the tour the nights closed in before we finished. We always waited until after we were due back to the logistics park to save ourselves from being pulled into whatever end-of-day hijinks our commanding officer was pulling. We would sit on the berm and look out towards Three Mile Hill and at the lights of a small village nearby. The call to prayer would echo from crackling speakers in the village and drift towards us – it was as eerie as it was beautiful. That noise seemed to make superb sense in the desert. It somehow suited the heat and the dying light at the end of the day.

Near our tents stood rows of phones. We would wait in line for our allotted weekly twenty-minute phone call. Our cards had a pin code that you had to enter through the keypad. All our calls were monitored and what we could say was strictly controlled. Whenever someone British died the UK phones and internet went dead. This lasted until the family of the dead soldier had been told. When they cut out we all felt dread that it might be someone we knew, then guilt when it was someone else. This was not nearly as bad for us as it was for our families. At home the TV would announce that a soldier had died and thousands of families would wait tensely for a knock or a call. Those who did not receive one then felt glad, and then guilty for being glad that it was someone other than their own who had died.

Gradually more equipment and men started to arrive in Kandahar. The mortars from outside the perimeter seemed to begin as a response. These night-time explosions became regular and sometimes hit inside the camp. The noise they make is hard to describe: they whistle and then hit with a thump-crunch. Our bangs, it was said, were the sound of freedom. So it made sense that, according to the logic of war our opponents' bangs were the noise of oppression. Either way our fear soon gave way to irritation. The alarms would stop and we'd return to bed, cursing. We called the offender the Rocket Man, after the Elton John song. The humour faded a little when one hit the dining facility during evening scoff and wounded three Canadians.

We started to be assigned guard duties on the gate, herding the jingly drivers to and from holding areas so their trucks could be sniffed by explosives dogs and checked over by their mercenary handlers. While on duty I made a point of trying to engage with the locals. Some spoke English while others spoke Urdu to our Ghurkhas. An ancient man showed us the gaps in his flesh where he'd been hit, apparently fighting the Russians. These Afghans were fine with us, the only time their demeanour changed was with the Americans who'd appear and bully the drivers, calling them ragheads and sand niggers and the like. I assumed the Americans had be trained in how to interact with locals, but many of them acted as if they had a divine mandate.

We had daily briefings reporting the deaths of 'armed men'. They were assigned different names like Taliban, militia or insurgents, but most often it was just armed men. I started to think about the vagueness of it all, though I kept it to myself. We'd been told that everyone in the country was armed. I didn't raise it at the time, because it seemed to be widely accepted that if you are armed, even in a country where everyone is armed, you're the enemy. 'Just get on with it,' was the mantra we had been given. And curiosity was out of my pay scale.

One briefing told us that out in the hills a group of armed men seen 'herding' a large number of women had been bombed with JDAMs, which are effectively very large aerial bombs. We had been told that women are always escorted in Afghanistan, particularly in traditional, rural areas. How were they so sure that these women were not being escorted? I had questions and I buried them as they came up.

The opposition leader David Cameron visited us during our tour. He wandered into the logistics park surrounded by heavily armed bodyguards and looked for the entire world like a public schoolboy in a war zone – leaking sweat and wearing cords and an outrageous shirt. We had worked all morning to set up stands for him to walk past: ammunition troop had mortar cases and ammunition boxes to show off, fuel troop had jerry cans to display and so on. He stared at us from between the ranks of his heavies, armed as they were with cut down, ninja-looking carbines. He gave us a look, which combined condescension with complete incomprehension. He kept a good distance, maybe ten feet, looked briefly at the products of our labour and then wandered off to see some more interesting stuff. He never said a single word to us and we all exchanged looks with each other in the burning sun. A *Daily Mail* report later quoted him as saying he was there 'listening, learning and showing our support for what is being done'.

These were some of the features of the American town they had built in southern Afghanistan around the strange arches of Kandahar International Airport. These big arches that looked like the McDonalds sign. It was a world of Americana, cowboys, bomb dumps, crunching rockets and thousands of young soldiers squinting and scrabbling around in the gravel.

Chapter 5

Questions were not encouraged. It helps if the people fighting or supporting wars don't examine them too closely. I broke this taboo one day. I had developed a cyst on my ear from years of being punched and kicked in sparring and it flared up in Afghanistan. Because of this our squadron's OC – an eccentric who stitched para wings to his dog's collar – demanded I win a Victoria Cross for him because a private at Rorke's Drift had done so when bedded down with a similar ailment. Winning a Victoria Cross was highly unlikely in Kandahar so I went to see the medics instead. I crunched down the road to the medical centre with my troop senior NCO. The staff sergeant was a bodybuilder – a book-smart, twenty-year man whose very soft voice was at odds with his massiveness.

I told him that some of my family had taken part in the anti-war demonstration in London. He nodded and said, 'Well, they are obviously people of principle and that's fair enough, not many people do agree with Iraq.' I got the impression that he hadn't been that keen on the whole thing himself. It didn't seem to add up that a soldier would not agree with a conflict. War was what we did, right? He told me how his first tour had been the 1991 Gulf War and how it had passed quickly divided as it was into guards, fatigues and rest. He said he had no illusions that the First Gulf War was about Kuwaiti children, rather it had been about oil and money and power. His frankness surprised me and I took it on board.

As more troops arrived and were sent from Kandahar to Helmand the war escalated. Our daily briefings informed us that the infantry soldiers were being pinned into the platoon houses (the fortified safe houses used as operation bases) by the insurgents and were denied any kind of movement. It was even perilous flying supplies in and bodies out, as the helicopters had to dodge enemy fire in key areas of Helmand that were more or less dominated by the Taliban. The guys coming back from the forward areas told us that it was a nightmare – they were being thoroughly outdone by the insurgents. There began to be talk of convoys or 'road moves', just to get people in and out. Until that point moving people and equipment had been done by air, but we were told helicopters were 'expensive'. I guess we were considered cheap.

In Kandahar, the Americans continued to do fascinating things. We had all seen movies where a platoon or company of US soldiers would jog in perfect time with each other, singing a soldierly cadence as they went. The reality was rather less impressive. One day as we headed for scoff, we saw a long column of soldiers coming through the choking dust. At the front was a soldier with a flag and alongside him a handful of the fitter troops jogged in some kind of order. Behind them, strung out and ragged, came a mob of overweight, staggering figures. As they went, they kicked up more dust and those behind them choked on it. They were a mess and it must have taken ten minutes for them to pass. We looked on as this odd procession disappeared from sight. The Americans, the lead nation under whose command we were working, were far from the crack troops they claimed to be. On the contrary, they were like us: mostly kids and hardly in fighting condition.

Being in Kandahar put us near UK headquarters and this meant that we could not escape the attention of the commanding officer of our regiment Lt. Colonel Smirnoff-McManus. At the ammo site we escaped some of this, but in the stagnant rear of the war no one could avoid all of it. Being in Kandahar seemed to affect many officers badly; it seemed to make them want to fuck us about in order to redeem their distance from battle. Every soldier in the camp – bar the stumbling Yanks – did their own physical exercise at section level. However, our CO decided that we were better than everyone else and therefore we would get up around five and do a lap of the airfield, choking in the dust every step of the way. People were going 'man down' on the roads and by the third week of this, half the regiment had reported sick, genuinely or otherwise.

His next brilliant idea was that because the soldiers in 13 Air Assault Regiment were better than everyone else we would tuck our shirts in. This was fine for the regimental HQ, which was air-conditioned but ridiculous that just for the sake of appearances we had to tuck in the shirts of our combats. Not the greatest hardship, rather it highlights a mindset. Especially given that these shirts are not designed to be tucked in. Eventually, in an inter-service argument the RAF – who ran the UK forces' medical centre – ordered that this practice be stopped as it meant everyone became unnecessarily hot.

This kind of thing was commonplace at the rear as bored, war-horny commanders took to messing everyone around for their own entertainment and trying to impose their own ridiculous regimes. After much posturing and chest-beating our senior officers would often roll over. Perhaps those types of situations were due to us being locked into this strange American town in Afghanistan, or perhaps it was just the normal kind of stuff all soldiers endure. It was my first tour and I had nothing to compare it to, but the old hands said it was quite routine.

The military even – or especially – during war finds ample time for bullshit, gratuitous willy-waving and arguments about whose train set it really is.

We had already lost a Chinook and wondered if we would end up doing road moves. One morning we drove out to the ammo site past the RAF Chinook detachment at the end of the runway where we saw one that had been badly damaged. It had been landed on wooden pallets because its landing gear had been shot off. Apparently, on some covert operation, it had landed in the mountains and been ambushed. Everyone had been ordered off into a maelstrom of bullets, then ordered back on and flown out. The helicopter had been bleeding fuel all the way home and eventually bumped down in Kandahar with its rattled crew and Special Forces team intact.

American soldiers asked us why this was such a big issue. They told us that when something broke they just sent for another one. Our equipment, on the other hand, had to be repaired and reconditioned. It would be great to have unlimited funds as they did. Later I was to get another demonstration of how wasteful the Yanks were compared to us.

In the laundries one day over a typical military conversation between some Brits and Americans regarding which nation's rifle would best survive being buried in the sand I got talking to a supply sergeant in the US Army. He was the first hillbilly I had ever met. He was about thirty, as mad as a bag of cats and had roughly four teeth. He was a friendly type and said if I ever needed anything I should go down to his supply depot and ask for him by his nom de guerre, Dirt Bob. Despite concerns that I might walk into a Klan meeting, I stumbled through the heat to his supply depot and asked him if he could get us any padlocks for our containers.

He then showed me the US Army supply system. It was like Amazon.com for soldiers but the bill was picked up by American citizens back home. They could get anything. And whatever they ordered was effectively written off and unaccountable once it was in theatre – from penknives to Humvees. We, by contrast, got charged for anything we lost. For example one of our privates, the hapless Dobbin, had lost a magazine of twenty rounds. Each round cost a few pounds, yet he was going to be charged the customary two hundred and fifty pounds for each one in the magazine until he managed to impress the CO on PT. I ordered thirty padlocks and picked them up a few weeks later. Bob had originally suggested a trade. We Brits had little to exchange, except box upon box of blue tissue paper. I avoided him for the rest of the tour, ducking out of the DFAC every time I saw him, even though the padlocks were pretty ineffective in the end. The sand jammed them. Like a whole range of things – Chinooks, rifles, imperialism, the US and British armies – they didn't function at all well in the desert.

Kandahar was the hub for repatriating our corpses: the dead were sent back there to be boxed up and shipped home. All nations would assemble their spare people to salute the Western dead onto transport planes. On our first repatriation we filed en masse onto the tarmac by the airfield. Then came the Americans, Canadians, Romanians, Australians, Danes, Estonians, even the baseball cap-wearing middle-aged women from the Tim Horton's – a Canadian chain of donut shops which had been flown in especially. It was an evening ceremony and the heat was still oppressive as we stood in long ranks and mocked the other nations' ways of marching. The

Americans were particularly slovenly, while the words 'left' and 'right' in Romanian sounded hilarious to us. We all had to salute as the bugler played and six soldiers carried the coffin up the ramp of the plane. In the background one of our lads, a Scottish kid who was sick at the time retched onto the tarmac between the tight ranks. Nobody said anything but the smell of bile rose and mixed with the hot air.

Our regiment's only casualty was a kid from another squadron. A sniper killed him as he left one of the forward operating bases in Helmand. The story went that a soldier on the truck in front of him had dropped his rifle and they had been forced to stop so it could be recovered. They stopped long enough for a man out in the desert to aim and long enough for the bullet to travel. It hit his mates hard. By this point we had become used to repatriations. We spent a lot of time on that tarmac saluting dead bodies.

The ammunition we were handing out was being used at an astonishing rate considering that one of the less vague justifications for the occupation was that we were peacekeeping. All I knew was that it would go as quickly as it arrived and we issued it as it was delivered. At one point the artillery had fired so many 105mm high explosive shells that we ran out for several days, and all we had left were the illuminating shells meant to light up the battlefield. On another occasion it became so busy we worked for a whole day and all through the night just stacking boxes upon boxes. We fell asleep on pallets of mortars to avoid the snakes. When the pallets were taken we slept on the cargo nets in the dust until the sun came up and it got too hot to lie there.

In May 2006, I left for R&R and I had my birthday at home where summer was glaring hot, yet still cooler and greener then Afghanistan. I hated being home immediately and wanted to go back. No one quite got my stories even when they asked for them. My friends took me to a pub and paraded the burned, brown hero. I drank too much Irish cider and vomited in the corridor of my mother's block of flats. I stumbled away like a wounded man to sleep it off.

All I knew was that I longed to go back to Afghanistan. I had started to question it by then. On the telly and the radio the same bullshit was repeated over and over again about how it was going well and about how we were winning, though it was the hardest fighting since Korea. But still I felt like I had to get back desperately before I had too much time to think about it. At that time the civilian world offended me and was strange, with its lack of mortars or helicopters passing overhead and the stronger-than-remembered booze.

By the time I returned to theatre the infantrymen were rotating back to Kandahar for their R&R, looking haggard. Many had been ordered to grow beards which was meant to elicit respect from the locals.

I wondered if by growing beards this would somehow conceal from the Afghans that we were occupying their country by force. The logic seemed to run that an angry Afghan civilian would emerge from his compound to confront a British patrol, only for his venom to disappear at the sight of their facial hair.

I was starting to question the whole thing. It seemed so stupid. I was jaded and pessimistic by the time I'd been back a week, but many more months still stretched out in front of me.

Despite obvious differences in budget from the US, our expenses were substantial. The Hellfire missiles alone cost £100,000 each, and could only be on or attached to an aircraft for a limited number hours because of wear and tear, and this included the flight from Britain. They only had eight hours of flight time left once they arrived and then became unstable, so they would often return to the our ammo site useless and scrawled with anti-Islamic graffiti by the loaders. I wondered what £100,000 could do to win the locals over to our cause, or educate children, or what it would look like in medical supplies – simple questions I had no answers for.

The locals fired rockets at us at a steady rate of one or two per week, sometimes several at a time. Occasionally the timers would fail and they would go off during the day. I was in our tent in the early evening when I heard the whistling. From the noise you could judge where the rocket or rockets were going and the noise was getting louder. I scrambled for my body armour as it hit and exploded. The alarm started wailing and shouts went up. I burst out of the back of my tent, which was surrounded by a barrier of gravel-filled steel cages to provide protection.

As I peered over it I could see the hit had been close. Through the dust, I saw two figures on the ground, I could not tell their condition, but I saw their civilian dress. I wanted to climb over the barriers and attend to them but I didn't know if there were any unexploded mortars lying in the sand and gravel. We had been briefed to stay in hard cover until the all clear. I watched them through the haze as the sirens continued to blare. We were called away for area checks.

I never forgot the image of those two figures. We were not guests, but invaders. We were not the friends of Afghan people, we were occupiers. Insurgencies, I knew even then, cannot survive without some degree of sponsorship by the population. The paras were being battered in Helmand. Insurgencies of the scale we were seeing cannot happen without popular backing. I did not have to be a general to recognize this.

There was a Nimrod crash five miles from KAF which highlighted the inadequacy of our equipment and the waste of lives. By the time a quick reaction force got there the crash site was being looted. The RAF regiment tried to form a perimeter, but they were few and were overwhelmed. We stored the coffins and when the bodies, or what was left of them, were brought back we delivered these caskets to the medical centre. The talk amongst the RAF guys was that the planes were old and that these men were dead because of equipment failure. It was no revelation. We referred to our own clapped-out Snatch Land Rovers as cardboard boxes and even our issued boots were of such bad quality that they ripped people's feet up. I bumped down the road in a forklift with the coffins stacked up on my forks, two or three at a time. I set the coffins down on the gravel outside the medical centre and helped the Military Police line them up. All I could think was that it was a waste.

By this time, I had started to question more and so had some others. I can remember chatting with one of my colleagues during a quiet spell.

'Why are we here?' he asked our boss who was passing by.

The officer shrugged.

'We are here…' I said, talking some shit, '…well, it's for the national victory, mate. To do good turns.'

Troopy frowned and the other guy laughed it off and went back to work.

The ammunition site was growing around us. The blast walls went up and the concrete was laid, while local workers fixed the hangar-like storehouses together. In the dust our missiles now sat in refrigerated containers alongside crates of Coke and Pepsi. We were down a man by then: Private Dobbin had been kicked out of ammo troop for being a liability. He had been handed around every other troop and looked like he might be coming back to us until he managed to cut off half a finger while adjusting a set of forklift forks. He was medevac'd back to Britain. Had he been American he might have got a purple heart for the wound, we conjectured, but he was British so we all ripped into him for getting an early trip home.

By that stage of the tour everyone was sick of it. Another guy – an extra body from another regiment – came out to Afghanistan, didn't like the look of it, went sick straight away and got medevac'd too. He got his medal, as well. This was not unusual.

There was a trend for officers – young and old – coming out for the qualifying thirty or so days and then heading off home for their medal. Our padre spent seven months on RAF flights – pinging back and forth between Kandahar and Essex in his effort to diminish our sins. He was not popular.

By then I'd started to accept that we had no good reason to be in Afghanistan and my increasing despondency affected my work. One night, while unloading ammunition in a forklift, it boiled over and I got into a row with our section's second-in-command. He got the drop on me and hit me straight in the chest. He was a Fijian and all muscle, and he put me on my back in the dust. I stalked away to the Land Rover and pulled my rifle out of the rack. I was severely pissed off and weighed up the idea of putting a bullet through him. One of the guys dissuaded me and I put the rifle away.

Paradoxically, I was reassigned to fuel troop and put on guard duty at the logistics park as a punishment for the crime of being hit. There was a regimental gathering and some of the lads smuggled me some beer and my head spun in the duty bunk, where my rifle and I had been relegated. Though armed and drunk I didn't resent the guy, he just got there first. He had a wife and kids and we got on most of the time. War-like environments make a person *shooty*, that's all. That kind of clash wasn't unusual.

Reports period came up and the brass worked away in their offices, writing about how shit or good we were. I got 'recommended', but had no idea what this meant. It was my first report so I took it to the lance corporal in charge of fuel for translation. 'You'll get promoted from that,' he said. I didn't believe him. 'Wait and see,' he added. 'It's all about the write-up they give you.'

Our troop commander had written that I was 'a mature, humorous, popular and intelligent soldier' who was 'proactive and out-performs his peers'. Apparently I organized and controlled others and was 'trustworthy and reliable'. My attitude, ability and confidence set me apart. I would make an excellent junior non-commissioned officer. The officer commanding, eccentric as he was, seemed to be my number one fan. 'An intellectual soldier; ambitious, smart, motivates his contemporaries. He has gained the respect of all ranks. He is recommended for promotion.'

It was almost funny. I had diminishing belief in what we were doing and yet had been rated one of the top privates in the regiment. When the OC was replaced later in the tour, his successor – an equally posh, if more grounded bloke – arrived and added that I '... worked hard in difficult conditions and high temperatures ... processing hundreds of tonnes of ammunition each week. Intelligent and mature ... he has a natural leadership style that the younger soldiers have recognised and look up to ...' You are never as damned as by your own words.

I was starting to put things together. The justifications for us being there appeared untrue. I never assumed a radical or political position. It was just a case of acknowledging that we really weren't helping anyone – certainly not the Afghans. If anything they were in the way of this project. Despite statements to the contrary, the 'chogies' were clearly considered

Untermenschen. Even from my limited understanding I could take a position on it. No one on our side seemed to know what they were doing. But what I did know was that millions of pounds were being spent, hundreds of thousands of rounds were being fired off, women were being bombed, locals were being alienated and people were dying.

Besides that, serious money was being made in some quarters. Half of our logistics park was filled by the private military company Kellogg, Brown and Root. They had better kit than we did and better pay. The rest of the camp was similar, with many civilians but also many military contractor-types with a selection of exotic beards, quasi-uniforms, guns and knives. War was an enterprise. Outside the wire, the locals passed the time firing rockets at us, while out in Helmand the infantry were being done so badly that they were locked into their little fortresses. We were not wanted there. It had turned out to be a sordid adventure, but of course, we just do what we're told. There is no space for questions. This was the Soldier Box and we were in it.

Our replacements started to come in: 3 Commando Brigade, Royal Marines. They were all burly and hard. Except the guys who replaced us directly, they were mostly army – a composite battalion drawn from different logistics units. They were welcome to it, we said amongst ourselves. Fuck them. We were Leaving on a Jet Plane. We even started humming the tune of the John Denver classic.

We trudged down to the airfield in the early morning, clutching our equipment and ready to go home. When we left Afghanistan I can remember sitting on the runway in the dark, body armour and helmet on. The plane pumped out chaff (radar countermeasures) as we took off, great flashes of light whipped past the windows. I knew then that I would never return as a soldier.

We had a few hours in Kabul – beds were set up for us on the floor of a tent-like hangar. We were told not to wander too far and we did exactly that as a reflex. Some of the European soldiers were having a party in another hangar with a massive video screen, terrible Euro-pop and free sangria. We tried our best to get drunk and shouted soldierly abuse at each other as we sharked hopefully around the German and Italian women. When the DJ gave us a shout-out for the hundredth time, and we still refused to leave, the pissed off German military policemen closed in on us and herded us back to our accommodation. We stumbled over each other in the darkness and lay there in our camp beds. An hour later we were woken and chased onto another plane bound for RAF Brize Norton. I slept fitfully on the plane. We stopped briefly at Dubai or Qatar or some other sandy place. I dreamt dreams which were full of glaring light and whistling rockets until our descent woke me above green Britain. I longed for the cold and the wind, and on arrival I got it.

Chapter 6

We got off the plane into the early parts of an English winter and after being transported from Brize back to Colchester we were held in camp. Those people in the battle group who'd been 'forward' went through 'decompression' in Cyprus. This meant they were locked into a military camp and given some booze, asked if they thought they had PTSD and then allowed to get drunk. At least, that's how some of our guys explained it afterwards. We got a brief talking to by our padre and were allowed to get straight on the piss. By way of post-tour nutcase screening we were told not to beat up the wife, take drugs or shag anything underage. In short, we were on our own. Whether due to budgetary restraints or inefficiency, we did not need to be 'decompressed'. Even one of our guys who had shot an insurgent through the face on patrol wasn't given decompression.

A few days later I was promoted. I was three years ahead of my career curve. I had received the glowing annual report from my seniors and was near the top of the top third of the regiment's privates. The guys who had done time griped about it but that was that. I hadn't been expecting this. I was off the whole thing and wanted to start my post-tour leave – and perhaps leave the army altogether. I was twenty-four years of age and I'd been in a field unit for around a year.

We were so raging for a drink we went wild for alcohol and music and females. Our regimental homecoming party was held on the same night as those of the other returning units, with bumper cars set up for the night. After a few hours in the free bar we descended on Colchester and got into a massive brawl with the artillery. That resulted in no arrests from our team and a good hiding for the artillery. The only serious casualty was me: eye gashed by a sovereign-ringed overhand right. I rolled off the dance floor gushing blood and then abused the paramedics until they'd had enough. MacDougal carried me up to the medical centre where a nurse glued me shut. Violence wasn't noteworthy in the army unless you got arrested.

The next day I went in front of the new sergeant major for some admin and he looked me up and down. This sergeant major was well thought of and, despite my concerns, he just eyed my battle scars and shook his head. 'Fucking hell, Corporal Glenton,' he said, 'there'd better not be any discipline coming my way.'

We were sent on leave and I returned home glad to be free for a while, torn between the wasted effort and the knowledge that I was a junior leader now.

The process of returning home is difficult. There is no one who understands or, at times, believes your stories. Even close civilian mates. They do not grasp the madness of tour, or the bullshit, or the anecdotes and so they seem to look at you funny and change the subject. You come to crave the end of your leave so that you can see and vent to your comrades, because only they understand.

While you've been away people's lives go on uninterrupted. Society at home is detached from the violence and upheaval of operations, while for you the buzz keeps buzzing. People slap you on the back and tell you 'well done'. People told me I'd changed like the whole thing was a rite of passage. They know war from movies or from the tiny, carefully vetted images on the evening news. I was torn. The army had recognized me and decided I was an 'intellectual soldier', and that I 'motivated my peers', and that I 'deserved promotion'. While that talk benefits the ego, my objections to the war were beginning to crystallize into something impossible to ignore. I disagreed with the conduct of the war, with bombing civilians, categorizing everyone as the enemy or simply as armed men, with the racism and the disregard for those people. I felt compelled to examine the experience as much as I could. I knew plenty of other soldiers who were easily as intelligent as me and I wondered how they thought about it.

I had been to Afghanistan and had come back. I looked back at the last year, what we'd been told, what we were doing, and I disagreed. There was no dramatic moment when I saw all my mates killed, or I realized in gritty close-up that the war, as an institution, was pointless, nor had I been made to kill babies, or seen my father-figure sergeant shot by swarms of enemies. I did not have to live in a bamboo cage for years until John Rambo saved me. That kind of image serves nobody but film directors. I did not need to be in a FOB or become involved in a lengthy firefight to reach this new position and to argue that would be fatuous; I just came to disagree with the war.

Later, when I was better read, I started to realize the overall justifications for the war were equally weak. I didn't just become a radical overnight. Lots of others seemed to think the war was stupid or at least dubious. My staff sergeant, my troop commander, some of the other privates had all seemed to think along similar lines at various points. I was responding to what I was learning, and no contract in the world could restrain me. I saw no justness in the war. The reasons behind it, as well as the way it was being fought, were to me lies and braggadocio and cant and hypocrisy. I simply had new information now and, just as simply, my ideas shifted. Happens quite regularly to all kinds of people, I gather.

On leave I went travelling with a civilian friend. I was so choked with dust and sand that I wanted to go somewhere green. I chose Central America: Mexico, Guatemala and Belize. I drank a lot – booze was cheap – and I indulged, sometimes just to sleep. In the five weeks I was away, I had begun to recall and worry over the mortar hit and the people in the dust. I missed the sense of urgency after so long on operations.

Me and my mate visited lost cities in the jungle, spoke terrible Spanish, chased señoritas and generally made a nuisance of ourselves. I returned with a tan, a wool poncho and a beard. MacDougal told me I looked like a fucking hippy.

When I got back into Colchester barracks after leave I was told I was being posted to a different regiment, this time in Oxford. I tried to contest this with HQ and failed. I was told that nearly all the privates who'd been promoted were being posted to the same place. It turned out there were about twenty of us going. Apparently this new unit was going on tour, but we wouldn't be expected to deploy because of 'harmony' guidelines. We couldn't deploy twice inside eighteen months. Several older lads who knew of the regiment told us it was a crap unit. They called it career death. On reflection – other than leaving my mates – I didn't really care. I just had to wait until I could sign off, serve my notice and then I was out of the army. I had come to a pretty firm conclusion by then.

I had increasingly tried to understand the war in Afghanistan, and I read books about it that were plucked from my mother's shelves, to learn what it was about from a different perspective. But I was left with more questions than I started with. My troop commander was also going to the same camp. Now a captain, she told us that harmony guidelines would protect us and I was determined to serve out my time quietly. Maybe get a real job. Maybe go to university. I wanted to do a job that worried me less than this one.

Chapter 7

Dalton Barracks were grim. The unit, at that time, was led mostly by twenty-year men put to pasture. The state of them, and the camp, was poor. The camp was an ancient, windswept RAF base. The squadrons worked in aircraft hangars which seemed colder inside than outside. I was asked if I wanted to deploy by our sergeant major. I didn't. He said this was 'fair enough' and because of the guidelines this was accepted. The regiment deployed and neither England's cold shittiness nor the promise of blood money overseas swayed me to tag along.

I was now on rear party, a skeleton crew which remains in camp during deployment. Our only senior rank was an obese alcoholic sergeant who stunk of booze from morning until around midday. He bullied the younger lads unchecked. The junior NCOs tried to protect the privates in a losing battle. This sergeant followed the few officers and warrant officers around like an old, loyal dog and we avoided him until he sobered.

My detachment from work and from friends had increased. The people close to me must have known because I avoided sharing my experiences or my views on the war. I didn't recognize this as post-traumatic stress at the time. I told myself that my tour had been so much easier in 'R&R' Kandahar and that I had no right to distress.

It would take years to learn that trauma is relative, and those on the front line (if there is such a thing in modern wars) do not have a monopoly. Trauma is no gauge of toughness. I drank myself to sleep which affected work. I had always been punctual and effective and this was slipping. I excused it well, avoiding discipline with bluffing and because my record was good. I was mulling over it constantly, hyper-vigilant, dreaming weirdly, losing my focus, self-medicating – but soldiers are told to shrug these trivial things off.

The dreams were at once vivid and indistinct. I didn't wake up shouting. Perhaps even in my trauma my mind rejected the cliché. But I would jerk awake and be unable to sleep again. As CIA manuals recount, sleep deprivation is a good way to break someone if you have the time. I had the time and it broke me. I recalled the whistling of the rockets, the dust around the prone figures, the scraping of the fourteen coffins onto the packed gravel outside the medical centre in Kandahar.

I asked for a six-month tour in Kenya to get out of camp and away somewhere else. This was refused but I got six weeks on a training exercise out there instead. We were to support the infantry while they prepared for Afghanistan. We flew via Cairo. While the planes refuelled we were locked into airport shuttle buses. We were not allowed to smoke, though outside the Egyptian ground crews peered in at us, cigarettes smouldering. We arrived in Nairobi early in the morning and flashed our military ID cards. Outside arrivals was a Kenyan policeman with a huge beret, trailing a rifle amateurishly in one hand under a yellow sign that said 'no soliciting'.

We smoked until a bus arrived and then drove us through slums to a Kenyan Army base shared with the British. There some of us picked up vehicles and the rest stayed on the bus. We travelled to Nanyuki sports ground, a way station for exercising troops, almost in the shadow of Mount Kenya. A gaggle of whores hung around the gates at night. We were told that they were riddled with AIDS and should be avoided. Two of the infantry soldiers ended up having to trawl brothels for the specific girls they'd bought to get them tested. I wondered what the charge for this extra service was and I hoped it was a lot. They were put on light duties and everyone from the officer commanding to the lowliest private called them the 'AIDS victims'. I felt no sympathy for them, but rather for the women.

We drove out into heat of the plains to deliver men and equipment to a remote camp. After many miles we curved in our inelegant Bedfords through sets of caltrops guarded by armed police. After that we were in 'bandit country' and the roads were dust and rock formed like corrugated metal. When we would stop or slow our convoy, stick-thin children would run from nowhere to beg for sweets. In flight they looked like little black swastikas, one of our blokes said. They would brawl in the dust over whatever we had pulled out of our rations packs. We went through a desolate little town named Archer's Post where we sneered at the hippy-looking NGO people we passed. These were people utterly unlike us and we disliked them on sight. They looked flaky and civilian, we were hard and lean and soldiers and this was enough. Then we turned into the bush and drove through dry river-beds and on and on, until we found a tented camp. It had been bulldozed clear by sappers (engineers) and surrounded by a high barrier of cut thorny bushes. Here the earth was red and the heat battered us.

The bush was often set on fire by the artillery, or sometimes by the small arms rounds being fired down the ranges. Whoever had nothing else to do had to beat out the blaze with paddles as the fire flushed game past them: snakes, gazelles and so on. We had LECs (Locally Employed Civilians) to hump supplies for us as if it were the nineteenth century and we were Cecil Rhodes's boys. We slept under mosquito nets and the LECs in low tents on the bare ground. They carried spears in various sizes: big ones, which they told us were for killing lions, down to little ones for the dik-dik, a tiny deer. Others carried ancient Enfield .303 rifles and wore ragged clothes that might have been khaki uniforms once. The whole thing recalled an imperial expedition. Part of Archer's Post burned down one night and the village's head man asked for help to rebuild it. Our officers scoffed at him, and by then I had assumed this was their default mode. Their request seemed fair to me as we were rich visitors, but it wasn't going to happen. There was a war to prepare for, we were far too busy learning how to liberate the inept, meek Afghans to help homeless Kenyans.

It was jagged country and the heat broke people. When some lads went down from dehydration the senior officers blamed out-of-condition troops, saying they were weak and lazy. A sniper went down, a man renowned for his fitness, and then the officers started to go down during their trips out to watch the troops. Unwilling to slate their own species, the senior officers demanded more water. We did water runs to a Kenyan base nearby, hooking bowsers up to our trucks and Land Rovers. The water was pumped out and treated with vile tablets which rendered it potable but plastic-tasting. The transport section – a mix of infantry and logistics – sweated through our days ferrying water, bangs, platoons of soldiers and men brought down by the heat as helicopters buzzed in and out of camp. The anti-malarials they gave us made us trip out like on weak acid. A whole camp of tooled-up, burning, stressed, tripping people.

My dreams were worse than before: the furry, growling nearby-things and the creaking, chitinous floor-things that crept through the thorny barriers around camp at night would enter them at will and fear would wake me.

Our single helicopter wasn't enough to do early morning safaris for everyone, medevac out sunburnt Ruperts (officers) and fly the CO around to make him feel suitably alpha male. The army hired another one, this one sleek and cool with a slogan down the side.

The Air Corps were very popular boys. Even more so when one of our drivers, a forty-year-old lance corporal, got into an argument with the biggest of these Blue Tac heads (so named for their beret colour), an otherwise friendly Jamaican. At the time, we were all in the bar in Nanyuki on a break from the bush. The air trooper said that the Kenyan prostitute our man had fallen in love with lacked virtue, and our man contested this, demanding recompense. The air trooper knocked him out cleanly and well and we all cheered. Then Boyd, a seventeen-year-old private, got in the way and took a hit too. There was a concerted boo. Boyd was a good kid, but dumb as they came. He had badly wanted to come on this Kenya trip so he could tell 'When I Was In' stories. These are a rite of passage for soldiers. Now he could tell people about When He Was In Kenya and got knocked out by a Smurf (blue berets again). Once he sobered up and the bruises had spread across his eyes, rendering him panda-like, he was visibly content. War stories are precious.

Out in the bush our only African soldier struggled more than any of us. He was a Zimbabwean who hated Africa. He had set his mozzie (mosquito) net up in such a way as to not repel animals, but to attract and trap them inside. We never knew how he did this so effectively, but he would cry out every five minutes and flash his torch wildly as if a lion were spooning him.

We left Africa hot and stained dust-red. My taste for foreign expeditions as a soldier had gone away completely. The trip confirmed to me that I wanted out of the army. I didn't want to spend another day occupying someone else's country – be it in Africa, Asia or anywhere else.

Chapter 8

When we got back from Kenya I was summoned by the drunkard sergeant in the hangar.

'You're deploying to Afghanistan,' he said.

'No, I'm not,' I said, surprising myself. My world shuddered. This wasn't going to happen. I was getting out. He looked up at me, perhaps thinking he'd misheard me. I didn't even have to think: 'Because I don't agree with it,' I told him.

He frowned like I had switched into Chinese. 'You don't have to agree with it,' he said.

I stared him down. 'We aren't helping those people,' I told him. My view on the war, hidden until that moment, welled up. 'This war is bullshit. We're just fucking up their country.' By then I had caught up with myself and felt slightly awkward. He took each word like a physical blow.

'It doesn't matter what you think, you'll do what you're told. You're a corporal in the British Army.'

The sergeant huffed, puffed and stamped. I knew there would be comebacks, but I had made my case.

'We'll see about that,' or similar, were the man's last words before he dismissed me.

For clarity, that unfamiliar sound was a moral objection being raised through the proper channels. I wasn't going back. I was done with that shit. I was unwilling. And, as it turned out, unfit. I was not suffering post-war blues. I was unstable, sleep-deprived and in the grip of illness. When I explained my symptoms to the camp doctor, he told me I had low-mood stress. By no stretch of the English language or the medical profession do nightmares and flashbacks come under that heading.

Thereafter the sergeant had serious beef with me. I don't mind vendettas, I have plenty of them and the army's internal politics run on them – it's almost Afghan in its honour-based irrationality. But I guess I was his latest target and being at particularly low ebb I struggled to deal with it. Over the following days he accused me variously of being a tour dodger, a coward and a malingerer. No other seniors approached me. I assumed he was keeping it to himself at that point, or he had passed it up the chain of command himself and they'd told him to work on me. He started to criticize me for everything I did. Sometimes he made sly digs, sometimes he would shout me down in front of the other soldiers. He seemed to be in his element, he seemed to be enjoying his new game.

I made no secret to my colleagues of the fact I wasn't going. I told them it was some administrative mistake and that I was still under harmony guidelines. It would be sorted out soon enough. I felt stupid for having argued the moral point, but it had been churning for a long time. I kept that to myself. Eventually I went to the acting sergeant major to complain about the harassment. He brushed it off and added, 'of course you want to come on tour, we want you with us. I'll be in charge.' None of that filled me with optimism. He said it with the smirk of a boy with a new Scalextric set.

I was granted an audience with the officer commanding and asked him about the harmony guidelines. I didn't want to go straight into my views on it. The sergeant's ongoing jibes were bad enough without our resident Fauntleroy joining in. He was a young captain – fat though not jolly – who was waiting to get out of the army. The rumour mill said he had a flash job in IT. He told me they were only guidelines, not rules, and could be broken and I'd had long enough to readjust. I realized they were determined to send me. I knew I'd get no further if I voiced my objections. I felt that they'd be laughed out anyway.

I was at a loss. I'd raised my issues with my chain of command. I'd told the medical staff about my symptoms and been ignored. What trust I had in my superiors – whom, I now realized, were highly paid idiots hired to look after us lowly paid idiots – was gone. The bullying did not stop. It's amazing now that I didn't just smash him up. The guy was deeply unpopular. I might well have gotten away with it. He was usually alone in his office, propped up in his chair, sleeping off the previous night's ale. I have envisioned it many times since – preference for peace notwithstanding, it would have pleased me. But when you are mentally low it's easy to be ambushed.

Eventually, I saw the sergeant major and OC again and complained about the constant attacks. I refrained from going into my moral objections to the conflicts, having been called a coward and malingerer when I had raised them before. I told them about the bullying and the OC said he would consider it and decide if action was needed, which I assumed in officer-speak meant 'I will do fuck all'. But he did worse than that. Within hours the sergeant had pulled me into his office and raved that 'the OC knows my character' and 'if you put a complaint in against me you'll be laughed at.' I couldn't believe the OC had told him. I went back to our acting sergeant major, who confirmed with the OC that he had told the sergeant and shrugged it off. 'I'm sorry about that, he shouldn't have done it,' he said. From then on I knew I could no longer trust my chain of command. I was on my own and I had enemies now.

We started pre-tour training and were assigned to troops of fifteen or twenty soldiers. I was made second in command of one eight-man section. We were ordered to start wearing desert combat uniform again. I had stuffed mine into the daysack I had used on tour. Both the daysack and the clothes still had dust and sand in them. I washed and ironed them and pulled them on. The walls seemed to be closing in around me. I had no choice.

But I did have a choice. I was unwilling to go back to that hopeless war, but didn't know how to fight back. I was being attacked from all sides. The social and political game in the military is medieval and there isn't even the veneer of fairness we have in the outside world, just absolute power. Furthermore, you cannot easily assess the limits of a person with a mental injury. With physical injury you can at least see that a man can't hold a rifle or run, but a mentally ill soldier can break at any point. He becomes a liability to his comrades. I knew of a guy in my corps who'd shot a colleague and then himself on tour.

I was now second in command of a section to which I could no longer contribute. Some of them were so young they would have to wait until their eighteenth birthdays before deploying. I did not want the responsibility, nor could I have accepted it honestly. We would also be deploying with some fairly odious characters. The acting sergeant major was a worrying character with glazed eyes and the two gruff sergeants both looked about sixty. They were rust-rigid and even announced to those kids that if anyone deserted they would be hung, which I knew was just bullshit.

I felt an obligation to my comrades – those kids – that could not be fulfilled by going back to Afghanistan. There were moments when I lapsed back into a mindset that said, 'Fuck it, I need to go, that's my job.' This is called the moralism, I learned years later. Flaky, empty, abstract, fucking moralism about honour, duty, integrity. It is cant and illusion. The people who talk about it, who want us to internalize it must think it's hilarious when we buy in to it. They certainly don't pursue it themselves. These are other people's ideas. All of those concepts have value, but not in the abstract and not in playing lackey.

There were other moments that were as powerful – the new burden of autonomous thought was getting heavier. I was morally opposed to the conflict and this was irreconcilable with going along with it. I had joined the army half meaning to help people, to do something to improve the conditions of other people's lives, not to occupy other people's countries under the pretence of securing in my own. Perhaps, I had been stupid to believe that there was anything moral driving the war. But that's what they sold to us along with the economic argument: three meals a day, job security, maybe some education. What had changed was that I'd started to understand it.

I had summoned up my courage and bitten back my shame to go sick and ask a doctor for a psychiatric assessment. The doctor was a colonel and as I explained my symptoms and suggested I was suffering from depression he sneered at me: '*I* will decide if *you* are depressed.' I was eventually notified that I had an appointment with a psychiatric nurse – it might have led to treatment but did not and even that was given grudgingly. The doctor had actually asked me if I was trying to get off the tour. The appointment was at RAF Brize Norton and the date was two days after we were due to deploy to

Afghanistan. Options were thin on the ground and I couldn't go back to the seniors – talented bunch that they were.

I was opposed to the war, so I took the hard decision. They had turned on me, so I turned my back on the army. Contractual obligations – which are meant to be two-sided – had ended. They had abandoned their obligations and duty of care. They were intent on sending me and I had no recourse. So I turned to thinking about where I could go and what I could do. I sat in my room, drinking so I could sleep, and during those nights I examined their version of 'the right thing to do' and my own. My version won. My version was better.

A sanctuary was needed. I had considered going AWOL in the UK, but I knew they would catch up with me. I knew I needed somewhere distant and cheap. I booked a flight to South-East Asia with a set return date for three months. A friend had told me it was cheap to lose yourself there. As far as I was concerned I was not obliged to go back to the war and they had no right to make me – I didn't work for them anymore. I flew out during a long weekend before we were due to deploy, with no idea where I would end up. My anaesthetic came free in plastic cups via pretty Emirates hostesses and that booze placated my fears for the future and my demons for the long flight.

Chapter 9

I got off the plane into the humid, close heat of tropical Asia. I made my way by taxi to the filthy, clogged Khao San Road full of foreigners. You could tell how recently they had arrived from how pale they were. I arrive pasty and in a philosophical state of mind. Once I'd booked into a Thai guesthouse down a shaded alley, I went looking to get beyond drunk. I sat and thought through my situation over cold beers. I put aside all thought of going back, at least not yet. I was a fugitive. I slept that first night under a spinning fan that pushed the hot air around the room. My thoughts moved between consequences and what to do next. At some point I managed to disconnect and drift off into broken sleep with the aftertaste of cheap beer in my throat and the high-pitched chatter of Thai spoken in the distance.

I left Bangkok after a week or so. I hadn't planned what to do as a fugitive, but I figured I might as well keep going. I headed to the north of the country to a place named Chang Mai. I found another little sweatbox room in a hostel and stayed for a week or so. The drink was cheap and useful. I had heard you could get a boat into Laos from near there and so I travelled to the river and the lines of vessels packed tight in together and boarded one up a precarious plank and headed down the Mekong. It was the wide artery of Asia and churned brown. We stopped for the night in a riverside village where the electricity cut out at six in the evening. I sat on a wide balcony with the other travellers – Irish, Canadian, Dutch and English – and looked at the river while an ageing hippy stoked weed and opium into a pipe made out of an apple and passed it round. We sat, drank and talked Irish, Canadian and British shit. The drivel of the drunk and stoned is universal. It doesn't need to make sense and it always sounds profound.

When I awoke it was with a start as the previous evening's chemicals cut me loose. We boarded another boat that morning and in the afternoon we passed the spectacle of a burning funeral pyre on the bank. The flames blazed high against the backdrop of green forest. Mourners huddled around the burning body. Soon after that we docked at Luang Prabang. The old colonial city looked pristine and white against the jungle. There was an affirming moment in that city that helped me see other people in their proper light again. Other people had become a sore point and I did not socialize well at that time. I lost my wallet on the streets and when I realized it was gone I searched for hours, eyes fixed on the pavement. My money and cards were lost. I was stranded in the middle of Laos, in a city with no embassy – as if going to an embassy had been an option, which of course it wasn't. Asking around, I gathered the only diplomatic mission was Chinese and I doubted soldiers from the Royal Logistics Corps were high on their defection wish-list. As I sat on the curb depressed and hopeless a small Laotian woman approached me. She had found my wallet and had walked around the city in the blazing Asian heat. She had tracked me down with the photo from my army ID. I was amazed by this and thanked her repeatedly. Laos is a poor country and the wallet had notes spilling out of it. She refused money. It turned out she owned a shop, so I went in and bought something. I just paid full price without haggling. It was a wonderful act on her part and gave me back both my means and my perspective.

After a week in Luang Prabang I needed solitude again. I headed by boat to a tiny village upstream. I had heard that the forests of Laos, like parts of Afghanistan, were heavily mined and strewn with unexploded bombs. These were another legacy of outside interference.

Here again the electricity went off as darkness fell and I played cards on the balcony of one of the crude, wooden hostels with a pair of Israelis. We swatted huge stinging insects as a villager lit candles and mosquito coils around us. The Israelis were everywhere in Asia. They seemed to travel in company strength, many recently demobbed from the army. These two had grown long dreadlocks and wore the same baggy, silken Thai fisherman's trousers which were so popular with travellers. It was trendy to affect the look of Thai fishermen for reasons I never worked out.

The guy with the best English was surprised I had been a soldier. 'I never met a soldier from England. Were you in Iraq?' I shook my head and told him I'd been to Afghanistan, uncomfortable with the topic. He went on to explain the worthlessness of Palestinians to me in a conversational tone. 'I fucking hate Arabs,' he told me. 'Afghans aren't Arabs,' I pointed out. He was amused. 'They are the same fucking thing, man,' he said. I left him to it as he broke into Hebrew, relating what we'd said to his friend who snorted and laughed with him. I was not like these men anymore. I didn't find it funny to talk about Arabs or Afghans or anyone in the way I once had, as if those people were worth less than us.

Down in the village square below us, sitting up on its base in the half-light was a battered American bomb. On inspection its markings had confirmed where it had been manufactured. It looked like an old 500-pounder, similar in size to the ones the RAF had hauled back and forth on little trailers between the airfield and their bomb dump. It served as a kind of monument for the village, like the ones at home: crosses with plaques that are stacked with wreaths and saluted by old men laden with medals once a year. I assumed it had long since been unearthed and deactivated. In the rain and soft earth, I was once told these exploding things migrate, following the course of monsoon streams, churned up by farmers and released from the grip of the roots by landslides to roll free.

Either way, I assumed it could not have been dropped far from this isolated village and I wondered if the little hamlet had been picked out on a map as a harbour for insurgents in some briefing room in Saigon or on an aircraft carrier in the Gulf of Tonkin. Decades later, Israeli and British soldiers would sit above it on a balcony arguing over the intricacies of Asian ethnicity. The warm beer and the crazy Israeli card game absorbed me and I did not think on it anymore. In a way at least this Jew was right: Palestinian, Afghan, Laotian, Vietnamese. They come apart the same when you bomb them and in that sense people really are all exactly the same fucking thing.

The next day a group of us hiked even further out. The Israelis had left early and we caught up with them bathing in a pool at the mouth of a cave, pulling leeches from the water. I sat in the shade as some of my group explored a cave nearby and I considered the difference between their army and mine. Their army consisted of a bunch of crackpot conscripts who passed the time guarding their walls, and bulldozing houses. But was my army really more professional or slick or particularly averse to that kind of thing? We were no different.

Me and a gaggle of Australians and Swedes left them with the leeches and hiked on through perfect, tiered paddy fields to an even more isolated village and there we stayed in bamboo huts on stilts. I would lie at night shivering and hallucinating, aching horribly. Somewhere up there in the north I picked up dengue fever. As I headed back, an Australian doctor, newly-wed and backpacking, diagnosed me on a narrow long-tailed boat as it careened downstream through white water, inches away from jagged spikes of karst limestone. I'd spent my time in the jungle tripping out and shaking with cold in the heat.

I got a bus south to the Australian embassy clinic in Vientiane and there booked an appointment with an old Australian doctor attached to the embassy. He had a shining Harley parked in the shade of the palms outside. He confirmed the diagnosis as dengue fever. He prescribed me nothing and told me to use repellent more liberally in future and to wear long sleeves. I kicked around the city and ate spicy Laotian food by the river. Despite the dengue I felt better. I guess being out in the bush hallucinating and shivering had done something to me. I decided I would go to Vietnam.

For a few days I hung around the Laotian capital. I got drunk by the Mekong with another Brit who was staying in my hostel. He introduced me to another traveller who was Vietnam bound. We plotted to do what the Americans had failed to do and reach Hanoi, albeit by bus rather than chopper. Dan had travelled from Brazil, where he'd worked in Rio slums and then on through Australia. His travelling arc went through South-East Asia then India. He came down the Mekong a few boats behind me. We drank ourselves into oblivion in a club on the roof of Vientiane's only modern hotel. The clientele were flip-flopped backpackers, dancing locals, elegant, pouting ladyboys and glowering pimps watching over their livestock. It was a seedy place and the soundtrack was terrible Laotian hip hop.

Our companion left for the islands. Me and Dan sat and waited with our bags for the evening bus to Hanoi. We sat

in a café by the Mekong. Vientiane had a small but conspicu-
ous African population towering over the local people. Maybe
they were embassy workers as Vientiane was where the
embassies were. The Africans were boomingly talkative, but
other expats stayed aloof from us transients and kept to their
own bars and their own company. As we waited, we decided
that if it was to be twenty-four hours on a bus we might as
well get drunk. We stocked up on Beer Lao and the toxic local
whiskey before taking a tuk-tuk up to the station where we
hung around some more. The locals laughed at the foreigners as we played up to their attention. The bus was cramped
and the seats seemed built for people two-thirds our size. We
crammed on and as soon as we got into our seats the aisle was
filled with bamboo mats and people sleeping on them.

At the rear of the bus we sat alongside two other foreigners, Malaysian travellers of Chinese extraction named Han
and Rohan. Han was sixty, retired and jolly and spoke British
English. He'd been raised on a remote little island and edu-
cated by a British Catholic priest, back when Malaysia was
Malaya. His nephew's English was less assured but still fluent.
We drank most of the night until we passed out. Through the
whiskey haze that descended, I realized that I was a modern-
day draft dodger seeking sanctuary in Vietnam, of all places.

We stopped several times on the journey. The first time, we
crammed into a shack on the roadside – it seemed to be like a
South-East Asian Little Chef. All eyes were on us foreigners.
I was quietly thankful that we had the two Malaysians with
us, I though it upped our street cred slightly. We ate whole
fish, impaled like lollipops on bamboo, and soup with bobbing
meaty lumps of animal flesh.

The second time, we jerked awake at a truck stop – in fact,
a truck stop and brothel combined. The driver wandered off
to get his rocks off in some dim parlour and left us to stumble

from the bus in search of food. We sat on benches by the road and waited for the driver to emerge. When he did he was doing up his belt.

We then drove along narrow roads beside sheer drops until we reached a border crossing in the mountains. It was an eerie place with karst peaks all around, one road in and one out. We were processed by the green-uniformed Vietnamese guards. Han, our mentor, encouraged us to bribe our way through, which we did. They had a system whereby one guard would linger over your passport, and then call another guy with more badges on his uniform. He would then look at it for a while before calling another man with yet more badges. This went on until you slipped them some currency.

We got into Hanoi and I belly-laughed there for the first time in months. Dan proved to be a good companion and there was much that was strange and funny in Hanoi. The city was polluted and the centre was maze-like, with hundreds of wires hanging off every lamp post, thousands of mopeds and a Wild West edge. The people here were fierce until they knew you weren't American. Many of the US travellers wore Canadian flags on their luggage. We toured the place and haggled over prices that were worth pennies at home. To not haggle seemed rude. We queued for hours outside a striking mausoleum to be ushered past Uncle Ho's elegant, reclining corpse. He looked truly solemn there with his wispy moustache and his palms across his chest. This strategist who had put great power to flight – I wondered what he'd say if he knew they were still at it and if he'd have felt any kinship to the Afghans or the Iraqis of today. The white-uniformed soldiers, crisper and smarter than British guardsmen, hurried us out to let others pass the wizened carcass.

Dan went his own way at that point and I headed south, escaping Hanoi's polluted anarchy. I was on my way to destruction by then and quite happily so. The drinking, my situation and the heat had made me happy-go-lucky. When things are very bad, I was beginning to find out, you could live life like you didn't really care.

I stumbled into Cambodia and went to the killing fields, where bones and clothing poked obscenely out of the ground. A sign by a single palm tree told us that in this place people were murdered by the Khmer Rouge, their heads sawn off with serrated palm fronds to save on bullets. I went to S21, a school which had been turned into a gulag by the Khmer Rouge. Inside, there was a simple black and white picture of a person chained to a bed – the last person to die there. And in the centre of the room were those very same chains arranged on that same bed frame.

As I left to board a tuk-tuk, I saw a disfigured man amid a group of others. It looked as if his face had melted and flowed away down his neck and shoulders. I marvelled at his injuries as we pulled away. That whole country was a place of scars.

I accompanied two Irishmen from my hostel to the local shooting range. This was a popular tourist activity and you could pay to throw grenades and fire off Kalashnikovs. I abstained. I knew enough about ammunition to mistrust bangs which had probably been kicked around since Pol Pot had been in charge. It was rumoured you could pay to machine-gun chickens or blow up a cow with a rocket-propelled grenade for five hundred dollars. There was nothing cool about firearms to me – they are practical, devastating things. They are tools, not toys.

After that I ventured north to Siem Reap and wandered around the temples there: the Bayon with its strange, eroding faces and Angkor Wat. I marvelled that all this had been done by manual labour, the great lakes and canals dug by hand. The evidence that people can create both wondrous and truly monstrous things is very stark in Cambodia, with its great temples and rusted beds and chains.

I was still a mess, but the distance and detachment had helped me to think on the future. I had told no one of my situation. I had sat silently in a hostel by the lake in Phnom Penh while more informed young people talked about the fallacies of Iraq and Afghanistan. I kept my views, radical but undeveloped, to myself. I wasn't ready to debate it, nor was I ready to return. I wasn't ready to fight that battle yet. But I decided that when I did, it would be on my own terms.

Chapter 10

I had been to Australia before but never to Sydney. Walking through customs was movie-scene tense. I had managed to obtain a visa with unexpected ease. I'd gone online and ticked a few boxes – the only question which had been a concern was the one which asked if I'd ever been in a military force or been trained in weaponry or explosives. I clicked no. The visa came through within a few days. I'd heard that Australia had an immigration policy like Nazi Germany, but I suppose I was white and English-speaking and had not come on a boat. I checked into a hostel in the red-light district.

Dan had put me in touch with some people in Australia, including a girl named Clare. We met after a few weeks and we drank the terrible Australian beer which tasted only of cold. It turned out she was on the run too, in a sense, having moved out for a fresh start. She worked in the legal profession, which I thought might prove useful. More importantly, she was good company. After a few weeks, I told her my story. She got it, but the military system sounds so ludicrous to civilians. She couldn't understand why they would make you go if you were opposed to it. She compared it to having a job out in the real world and being asked to do something you didn't agree with – you'd leave. Why would they want to hold on to people who no longer believed in what they are being told to do? She was right. Why would you want to take someone with you who had objections? I guess that's why the military are always parroting lines like 'mine is but to do and die'. Well, fuck Tennyson.

I still didn't have a solid plan. I still kept my distance from people and found it hard to engage. They would ask me about the army and I would deflect their questions. I really didn't want to talk about it. I was in a difficult position because although I was aware of the shortcomings in the system I maintained my sense of loyalty to my mates. I didn't try to contact them because they might have gotten in trouble if it was found out.

During my time in Australia I was in limbo. I carried my secrets quietly but they were a burden. It is uncomfortable to view yourself as a deserter and sometimes I did just that. Of course, the truth was that I was only a deserter according to a set of one-dimensional rules that had been tailored by the other party to suit them. The military had done its job of indoctrination well, but not so well that I couldn't unpick it. The army has its traditions and I had found diverging ones, much like the deserters and draft dodgers who had fled to Canada and Sweden in years past, only I had ended up here. The modern United States is in part built by draft dodgers who fled imperialist wars in Europe. It was a historical endeavour to be on the run.

It was a hard road, one upon which I was alone except for Clare. We came to love each other and in Australia she helped me to heal. My family and friends were far away. I was still suffering from PTSD and would wake up at night, in turn waking Clare as I shouted in my sleep. She stuck it out admirably. I would sometimes think about what to do, but an urge to avoid it would soon creep in. I would find solace in the length of time left on my visa.

I was loose in the world without the support of my comrades, in exile on the other side of the planet. After the closeness of comradeship, the isolation was hard. I realized why soldiers cracked up after leaving the army. The things you talk about and the way you talk about them do not fit into the wider world, the world detached from jargon, excessive swearing and the physicality of the lifestyle.

Clare proved to be a good influence and I resisted treatment. I still do. For me there's a sense that it would tax the anger that was and still is my motivation. It still eats sometimes. But as I began to make a more serious effort to examine the situation, I improved. Thinking independently was good for my soul. It was liberating.

The year was passing quickly, and in order to apply for a visa extension of one year I had to go out into the bush and work for three months. I chose to be a farmhand over fruit picking. I got a bus out to a place called Trangie and worked on a farm a few miles out in the bush with a heat-maddened farmer named Gifford. Farmer Gifford had built a beautiful wooden house on the prairie for his wife and kids. His wife had since left him and his kids had all gone to Sydney. The place was like a graveyard. I couldn't blame his family for leaving – he was a fucking maniac and the desolation had bleached out his capacity to co-exist with anyone, let alone an anti-authoritarian pommy. For a while I herded his cows, learned to ride a motorbike and spent six weeks fixing punctures. George was waiting for the rain to come so he could plant his crops. This was why he'd hired me. It didn't rain before his cabin fever got too hard to deal with. I left him to it without regret.

I completed the necessary number of days on another farm, run by a younger farmer and his English wife. From the state of the accommodation it had last been used by convicts. In the approaching winter the nights drew in. There was little heating and no showers. It was like being on exercise in Brecon.

When I got back to Sydney it still affected me when people talked about the whole intervention in the Middle East. In any given crowd there always seemed to be a majority against and this surprised me. It seemed obvious to anyone who was moderately informed that the whole thing was built on lies. When I had come across these kinds of people as a soldier, I could return to camp and laugh about them with my mates. Out in the real world though, there were no comrades to slap me on the back and mock the stupid, liberal civilians.

I had become an expression of the war: irrational, contradictory and skewed with upside-down ideas, looking for legitimacy where there was none. When I did talk I often took that odd right-wing anti-war position that the principles of the conflict were right, but just misapplied. Or I would say that our rationale was this and that, regurgitating all the popular 'realist' justifications of the day.

I started to read a lot more in Australia – about history and that arcane thing called politics. A pattern unfolded: everyone from the Romans through Hitler and beyond had claimed a civilizing or a humanitarian mission at one time. Reading history confirmed what I had seen. The mission in Afghanistan was no more about security, freedom and liberation than about monopolizing the dish-dash industry. The myth was part of the Soldier Box. But I was discovering that the ideas that exist in the box cannot survive outside it.

Clare and I talked about it. She told me she thought I had been betrayed and cut loose. She was a rock throughout. I considered what I should do. I had unfinished business. I looked up the AWOL hotline. It's called that. A phone line set up for absentees. I stared at the number for months, scrawled on a Post-it note stuck to the wall above the kettle.

For a time, I was absorbed with revenge. The longer I stayed in Australia the more this angry desire was replaced by a more balanced wish for justice. I had loved the army, despite the Afghan adventure being so skewed, or at least I'd liked the people and I missed the fellowship it had brought. I felt that the option of force should be available to defend people's lives and liberty but my war, this so-called War on Terror, wasn't about that. I now understood that the military and its hedonism and its manufactured narratives were addictive and designed to separate you from the world. It dragged you back in and the call to arms – the hero myth – did not subside easily. My fight was never with the army in the sense of my fellow lackeys, but with the establishment who had despatched us, and those anonymous people who'd misused us. I started to understand that very few of my actual enemies live in villages in Afghanistan. I had started to become conscious and I had found ideas and arguments that seemed to explain what I had seen and felt.

I rang the hotline and made contact. It was a big step and I made it breathlessly. I didn't tell the man nestled time zones away where I was. I asked him about potential sentences. He spoke about desertion and AWOL and so on. He even asked me if had I ever lived in Australia – I guess I'd picked up an accent. I asked him if I'd have to serve out my time, though I knew I would make a fight of it if they tried to make me.

I talked to Clare about going back. She was a settled, permanent resident but she said she would come with me. I could have stayed, if I'd secured the right visas and sponsorship. But we wanted to make a life together. I have made many leaps of faith, but it was her leap that was most empowering. I had

some more time on my visa so we decided we would wait until
it felt right.

Since I'd done my agricultural work I'd been working
for a landscaping company and we built a path through the
affluent suburb of Cremorne. British soldiers are carefully
conditioned to scan and envy other people's kit, especially
when labouring under the hot sun in foreign places. This is
how I met Norman. On the path we were building I saw his
shitty, tan combat boots and took him for a soldier. He had a
strong Essex accent, an occasional stammer and resorted regularly to soldier-isms. He was an Iraq veteran and had left the
army and come to Australia with his partner Carla – a robust
Scottish woman with a brilliant, savage wit. Trained as a tree
surgeon, he had abandoned it in Australia for fear of arboreal
funnel-web spiders which can kill with one bite.

He told me he had spent his first day as a landscaper in forty
degrees, digging up tree stumps in Botany Bay like one of
the original convicts to these shores. We became friends and
I liked him like a brother. He replaced the comrades I could
not speak to and together we joked about the alien country
we'd found ourselves in – we even termed the confused
Australians we worked with chogies and marvelled at their
peculiarity

I did not tell him about my objections or my going AWOL.
Those belonged to me alone. Nonetheless, we spoke at length
about the stupidity of our wars and we shared stories of the
better times we'd had as soldiers. Like me, he thought the
wars were foolish but he clung romantically to the things he
had been told. I couldn't really criticize him there, as I had
once been the same. By then, these ideas appeared infantile to me and I bit my tongue when he echoed propaganda.
His strange, mixed consciousness was framed weirdly by his
unexpected house-proudness and skill at baking.

We drank each others' beers and I managed to ignore his politics because beyond them he was a decent man, and like me he was a little ruined. The main difference between us was he was still gripping onto the lies he'd been told and wishing they were true. I have met many good men since who desperately hold on to this stuff. I get it, especially if you have laboured under a lie, or maybe lost your friends or been damaged. We are all guilty of entertaining fantasies once in a while – this does not necessarily take away our goodness, but rather some of our usefulness.

We finished building that path in Cremorne together. Our bodies were long unused to such soldierly work and we ached from barrowing and digging and pounding bitumen between the concrete edges we'd put in. I don't usually go in for soppiness, but for me the path we built led back home.

By then I was much stronger. I felt I had the army's measure, and contact with the AWOL hotline had buoyed me. It's easier to marshal strength when you know what you are facing. Clare and I decided to get married and we had the ceremony by the Harbour Bridge in a little place named Kirribilli, with the opera house in the background. Norman and his partner were witnesses for us. I hate public speaking and I mumbled the whole rite nervously. Luckily, the rain held off until just after we'd finished the photos. We booked flights home and when the day came, Norman and Carla dropped us off at the airport. We boarded the plane home. There was to be no crawling back. I would fight as well as I could.

Chapter 11

We seemed to circle Manchester for days. I felt like I should have my helmet and body armour on. The longer it took, the more trapped I felt. I was torn between the years-long urge to come home and fight my corner and the fear of being snatched at customs. Eventually we started our descent and touched down. I was home, but not clear. Approaching customs, Clare leant in and said, 'I won't let them take you away.' We exchanged glances. The woman behind the desk seemed to examine my passport for ages. She looked over it and then glanced up at my face one last time and ushered me through.

I was back and unready. Fighting the temptation to hurry, we got our bags from the carousel and moved past the policemen in the arrivals area. We wandered out through the last set of doors to be met by my mother and uncle and Clare's sister. We left quickly. The adrenalin settled down after we reached my uncle's house. It had been raining in Sydney, but Manchester was burning hot.

Should I have come back? I had no idea what awaited me. I felt like a young soldier about to go on tour. As we sipped beers and I met my young cousins for the first time, I managed to set aside my concerns. I could handle it. Unless I was caught beforehand, I would go back to the army voluntarily and face them. There would be no skulking back: I was here to settle something bigger than a mere AWOL charge. This was a matter of duty, though not the army's half-cocked, narrow version. I had a duty to try and expose and hinder the war effort.

We headed back to York. I hadn't been there for many years and it was resplendent in summer. We spent two weeks there before I made the call. I rang the barracks and explained that I was coming back. We drove down to Oxfordshire the next day and Clare waited in the car as I walked through the gate of Dalton Barracks. The soldiers on guard ushered me in and I saw one of the lads from my old regiment in the guard-room. 'Where the fuck have you been?' he asked. It broke the tension of two years spent wondering about this moment. 'Unpaid holiday,' I told him.

The camp was still in a shit state: there was now a plague of rats and the hot water was going off for two weeks at a time. There was a small rear party as the rest of the regiment was in Kuwait recovering the last of the British military's equipment from Iraq. I was given my equipment back. It had been boxed up and put into stores for two years. I was told to report to regimental headquarters the next morning, and upon waking I got into uniform for the first time in two years and six days. I surprised myself by remembering how to iron it. I was told that I was free to come and go because I'd returned voluntarily. The adjutant explained I'd been charged with AWOL, and asked me if I wanted to stay in the service. No chance, I told her. It was time to get a grown-up job.

One of the guys I had known before my absence picked me up from the headquarters. Jimmy was a skittish corporal who had gone to Afghanistan before I went AWOL. 'Well, it was a shit tour anyway, mate.' He laughed when I told him where I'd been. 'Fucking hell, mate. You'd be a corporal by now. Why'd you go AWOL? Was it that fucking alcoholic sergeant?' he asked. I laughed, remembering. 'Kind of,' I said.

Back in the hangar it was a skeleton crew. I was introduced to the new sergeant. He was a pug-faced little man with a good line in racism. I took to him immediately. I even started to enjoy being back – it was a good group of privates and junior ranks.

The next day I was sent to see our acting OC. I banged my heels into the floor outside his door and saluted.

'Who are you?' He asked.

'Lance Corporal Glenton, sir, back from AWOL,' I said.

He nodded approvingly. 'Right then. Where did you go, Corporal?'

I paused. 'Australia, sir, for two years.'

He snapped up. 'Fucking hell, Australia! That is a *fucking good effort*, Glenton.'

I was back in camp and working as before, surprised I was not locked up. After the initial ease of returning I heard the old racist script again. Our diminutive sergeant took a particular dislike to one Ghanaian soldier who worked with us. He would snipe at the African constantly, making a point of stopping him from going on leave back to Ghana. The kid eventually complained, believing the attention was racially motivated. A huge row kicked off between the two of them.

Afterwards, when the junior NCOs were all sitting in our crew room, MBE marched in. We braced ourselves for a bollocking, but he paused, surveying us – presumably to make sure we were all the right colour – before launching into an astonishing tirade: 'Fucking niggers shouldn't be in the army.' He told us that we should discipline the blacks whenever we could, but that particular kid was his. In that moment I remembered what the army was really about. I had forgotten how profound the divisions were in race and class. I said nothing. I had my own shit going on.

I was taken to the military courts in Bulford and waited there to be seen. I wasn't sure what was happening, so when I was left in a room with a probation officer I was flapping. Nevertheless she interrogated me and I told her half the story, avoiding the issue of my moral objections totally. The memory of being attacked was still an uncomfortable one and, whoever this character was, there was no way I was going to spill my heart out to her. This was a war of position and manoeuvre.

When we got in front of a judge later on in the trial we raised the question of why, before even being sentenced and before even meeting my solicitor, I was required to carry out a pre-sentence report which was then whisked away for god knows who to look at. Pre-sentence, in my understanding means pre-sentence, not pre-trial. We were told this happens because they assume people will plead guilty and so it makes things easier. Pure army logic: we'll just assume guilt, they must be guilty, because if they are not it means we are wrong, which is highly unlikely.

My appointed solicitor appeared uninterested. He was a slovenly and condescending man who told us he'd been in the navy until he'd fallen out of a helicopter over Malaya. I almost clasped my head in my hands at this. He spent most of the time in our only meeting labouring over his shit war story.

I told him about the bullying but abstained from telling him about my objections. I got the impression he was the military's man, which added to my sense of foreboding. My heart sank as he effectively suggested that I just plead guilty. He seemed to think it would make life easier. At least, for him.

I went back to camp and rang Clare. We talked it through at length and were both concerned. Perhaps I should have told them fully about my ethical concerns, but I'd had my fingers burned before and I had no illusions about trusting them. I was angry about the whole thing, and angry at myself for holding back. I wanted to expose them and I wanted to make the stand I'd spent so long thinking about, but I held it all back under pressure.

When I'd first gone AWOL, my mother had urged me to talk to John Tipple, an old family friend and something of a firebrand. He was a legal caseworker and was exactly who I needed to speak to. I got in touch and he was as I remembered him: a straight-talking wrecking ball. The prejudiced and the arrogant generally crumble when they encounter him. I'd been going through the process of joining the army when I first met John in Ipswich. He'd asked me if I was sure about it. The question never even registered at the time – being wide-eyed and twenty-one and nearly gone for a soldier. He had a deep-seated concern for the downtrodden which, as fortune would have it years later, was me.

Unrepentant, he vocally opposed the army's hypocrisy from the start. When I sketched him a picture of the bully-ing and the legal process so far, he seemed unsurprised. In truth I had never met anyone who was harder to surprise – he was unflappable. He represented soldiers often and was apparently banned from Colchester Barracks. He told me that I should continue with the current lawyer to test him out. 'Don't plead, don't sign anything,' he said. 'They expect you to roll over, don't do it. They have a duty of care and they will bury you trying to cover their fuck-ups. For now, I'll be your silent partner in this.'

I rang my assigned solicitor and demanded a meeting, telling him that I was going to be taking an active part in this defence. I needed to know I could trust him before I got down to the facts. He told me how busy he was and I explained that, legal aid or not, he was working for me. He conceded in the end and I told him I wanted to meet my barrister as well. When I went to his office he was hours late, and the sour receptionist tried to bluff me, telling me I must have got the time wrong. I hadn't. I raged at her until she got in touch with the absentees. The barrister turned up without the solicitor and I was forced to repeat what I'd told him. I told her I would be putting in a not guilty plea. She seemed taken aback and said almost everyone pleads guilty but it was my choice. By the end of that meeting, to which the solicitor never bothered to turn up, they had both been found wanting. I didn't want my case read on the day of the trial over a Frappuccino on the train from London. I needed a brawler in bruising form and those two didn't come even close.

Chapter 12

When I related these events to John, he gave me some advice: 'Sack him, Joe. He's fucking about. I'll take your case.' John had been on a sabbatical from legal work, but was willing to come back for my case. I got in touch with my assigned law firm. The solicitor was out, so I left a message: 'It's Joe Glenton. Tell my solicitor he's sacked.' And then I hung up. That was that.

As soon as I tried to transfer the legal aid, the armed forces legal department tried to block it. I argued with them all day, pouring my venom into phones and fax machines. They told me how wonderful and efficient my ex-lawyer was and how I'd have to explain what was wrong with him in depth. 'No, I don't,' I told him. 'I can be represented by anyone I choose and this guy can't even turn up for meetings on time. I'm sacking him and replacing him.' He dragged his feet all day long, eventually coming up with some bureaucratic whimper about the public purse. John faxed him and told him that he was blocking my chance of proper legal representation. John asked him what was more important, justice or the public purse?

The legal aid was duly shifted to John's firm. I had found my scrapper. 'Joe,' he told me, 'this is going to be a white-knuckle ride, mate. It's a rollercoaster. You've got to stop at every watering hole and Joe, write everything down. *Everything.*' He quickly found me a barrister named Nick Wrack to replace the Frappuccino sipper I'd been given previously. He was a scrapper as well. And even better, the army itself would be paying for John and Nick to savage them.

Soon after, the charge was upped to desertion. It is a more serious charge: desertion is AWOL with either an intention to remain away forever, or the intention of avoiding active service overseas. They'd decided that I'd been warned off for a tour and had done a bunk. It was a gross oversimplification, but being overly simple is the only thing the military does consistently. The fight rose in me again when I got the new charge sheet.

Both sides were starting to shape up for the fight. They were trying to rattle me: ten years or more in prison for desertion did not look inviting. But I felt like I was doing something decent. Or maybe I was trying to get back a sense of right and wrong. Maybe it was irrational, but it made sense at the time. I was in a state of insurrection and I liked it despite all the fear.

I met with John again and we discussed the case. After we'd talked through some of the legal trivia, he told me that those people who were trying to put me away only ever look big, until you get up off your knees. This became a mantra for me. I considered doing something publicly but this brought its own worries. Not least, because I'm a very private individual.

'Would it help to politicize this more?' I thought out loud. John considered this for a while, then said, 'Joe, it's already political. Do you think they give a fuck about you, or about those dead blokes, or those dead Afghans? Do you think they care that that bloke fucking turned on you when you argued with him? No chance.'

He had a point. It was really just a matter of tactics. The army is terrified of bad press. I had known that from the warnings we'd been given about the media at Deepcut and in our pre-tour training. The army hated the media.

The army wanted me to go quietly, but that wasn't going to happen. We had been lied to and deployed into a war for vested interests. I was no longer naïve, I was hardened: two years of exile and reflection had allowed me to think freely. I was also angry and sharp and willing to fight. I would state my views and go at them as hard as I could. I doubted I would win in the sense of a final submission but I was not a deserter. Cowards don't stake their liberty on anything, or take on governments and bruise them. If it was going to be prison, I wanted it known exactly why: because I had refused to return to war. I was in a position of some strength, precisely because I was a low-ranking soldier. It would be glorious for a scumbag lance corporal to have it out with a government.

I was interviewed by a leftist newspaper. It took two weeks for military intelligence to find it. Once they had seen the article, I was sent before our major who asked if I'd been tricked into it and I told him my case was none of his business. He told me that 'these people' are against whatever the army does. So far, the socialists I've met are more pro-soldier than the officers I know. Being pro-soldier is not the same as being pro-war.

Outside his office the hangar was in chaos. The rumours were going around that I'd been charged with treason and would be shot or hung or sent to the tower. The guys I worked with patted me on the back – I had been the quiet man. I wasn't quiet anymore.

My first radio interview was with the BBC. Clare and I then made our way down to a Stop the War meeting in London. I was scared; I have always been scared of being on display. We sat and drank coffee near the meeting place and it made me feel sick. Clare made sympathetic noises and John switched from mentor to sergeant. He had been drilled out of the army for being outspoken. And now what he said was passionate and more compelling because it was unrehearsed. He wasn't speaking as a lawyer, but rather as a good soul. I decided to carry out the act and I recognized that I was then a revolutionary in my own embryonic way. I chose to fight and I meant it when I did it, and I still hold to it now.

We finally went to the meeting and I almost tripped up when we got there. I was terrified by the amount of people gathered, and the idea of getting up on stage. Outside, we were met by Chris: an activist, tall and stooped and soft-spoken. He was with another man, who was shorter, wiry and bearded, an ex-SAS whistle-blower who had resigned rather than continue to render Iraqis and hand them to the Americans. He knew about this stuff and his posture said he was a soldier. My coming had been made known and I was ushered into the blur. On the stage, I looked out and each bobbing head was a point of trepidation in a sea of fear. Would I be arrested? I sat beside a woman named Jane Shallice. She told me that when they announced a serving soldier would be speaking she had just thought: *Why?*

My speech was hopelessly mumbled. I suppose the point came across because people stood and clapped. Malalai Joya spoke after me. She was a small, tense and striking woman. Her English was wonderfully accented and it somehow made her sound even more right. 'You should not apologise, Joe,' she had said during her speech, turning her dark, sad eyes in my direction, 'it is your government who should apologise to *you*.'

She was no fool. She spoke as an Afghan woman – and she was saying that it was precisely these women who were being used to justify imperialism at its worst, Afghan women being one of the most betrayed and lied about groups in modern politics. What she said made it clear to me that if we are stupid enough to entertain the idea that imperialism is in the business of liberating women then it follows that they are our Helens and Kabul is Troy. This is myth.

In the army the word for myth is bullshit. There isn't a soldier in history who's ever been briefed to kick down the door of a cowering family and burst in shouting, 'Has anyone got any unresolved women's rights issues in here, you mother-fuckers?' It's just not in the creed, so don't even try it.

A woman in her early thirties, Malalai is harassed day and night in her own country, a survivor of repeated attempts on her life after shaming a number of warlords, war criminals and drug barons in the new post-invasion Afghan parliament. Needless to say, she was something of a fireball and she became an MP at only twenty-four years of age. The Karzai administration, whom I had been sent to bolster, who some had been killed defending, were as bad as the Taliban, she told us, despite being the recipients of US approval. That day a fundamentalist mob had arrived at her accommodation intent on murder. She refused US guards and used Afghan soldiers instead. She still lives in hiding.

A few weeks later, while the army tried to figure out how to face my defiance, I handed a letter in at Number 10 addressed to Gordon Brown. The experience was terrifying, especially the media circus. Standing in front of reporters I asked for the withdrawal of British troops from Afghanistan. I did a lot of interviews and then went to the MOD building where a camera had been set up. Two senior officers waiting to be interviewed were both pushed down the list with our arrival. The line failed but it was worth it just to see the looks on the officers' faces. The next morning we were on GMTV.

When I got back to camp the regimental clerk, a red-haired Welsh sergeant, asked me if the presenter on the show –

Penny – was nice. I told him she seemed lovely, I guess he had a thing for her. He also told me, quietly, that he thought I was bang-on about the war even as he sorted out my disciplinary paperwork. He was a good guy.

The junior ranks – the privates and corporals – loved it back in barracks and a group of them gave me a round of applause. Our sergeant told me that I'd made it up, that I'd changed my story.

'I never told you my story, sergeant,' I said.

'You betrayed the lads,' he countered.

I looked over to where the privates and the NCOs were laughing about the whole thing. 'Find me an interview where I say anything negative about the lads,' I suggested.

He sloped off, grumbling to himself.

It was a strange time, in which I was a junior NCO in the British Army by day, and arguably the most high-profile anti-war campaigner in the country in the evenings and on weekends. I travelled around the country to meetings, did radio and newspaper interviews and answered the same questions again and again. In those meetings I met all kinds of folk who treated me very kindly and encouraged me in my task.

Because I had returned voluntarily, the army couldn't touch me at that point and apart from dragging me into some squirming senior's office a few times a week there was little they could do. I told them the same thing every time: I was conducting my defence and they didn't get a say in it. The reaction from the brass (officers) was seismic indignity. Of course, they couldn't really slate me because they were telling everyone how important and wonderful and fluffy the troops were. Senior officers and politicians had said themselves that the conflict was being messed up, though they hadn't gone as far as to say it was a complete and total debacle based on a pack of lies.

I was happy to address their oversight in as many interviews as I could, because in the military it's all about teamwork. My tactics had been spot on and the MOD PR machine had been taken into an arena where it could not function. Their options were limited, their unhappiness immense and the publicity stung them. Apart from the weekly bollockings and increasingly regular pre-trial hearings, they were scuppered. Toothless.

An email account was set up which was swamped with messages of support. We counted around three hundred positive ones to every negative one. Bizarrely, someone added the address to the BNP email so we had a regular and weirdly informative newsletter from them as well. They had also adopted a strange anti-war position. Presumably so they could bring all the troops home and use them to defend England from their fictional, idiotic caliphate. I do not know.

A number of groups sprung up online to oppose and support me. The positive ones were very kind and said I was a hero; the negative ones had a hilarious take on factual accuracy and half-cocked critiques based on not very much at all. They were riddled with far-right commentary and talk of fatuous things like patriotism and Englishness and my affront to them. It was all cowardice versus bravery and other narrow, moralistic nonsense. Individual resistance is terrifying and shows a willingness to fight if nothing else, and it cannot be reduced to fear or explained through name-calling.

I scanned the groups and found nothing to sway me. Among the greatest of the accolades my struggle brought was the anger of these hopeless folk. I rediscovered a love of annoying fools, which a soldier must bury while serving in the military. Some of these people seemed to have no words of their own and so they spoke in borrowed terms. 'The nation this, queen's shilling that, white feather this, queen and country that,' they sobbed. The truth is I was never really trying to convince those jingo-addled Morlocks. That they had to untangle themselves from their swinging tyres to press 'post' is a testament to the emancipatory potential of social media.

As for yapping about duty and honour and the Queen, it doesn't help anyone to try and analyse the world today with the vocabulary of a Flashman novel. I didn't send any soldiers to Afghanistan, perchance to die, for nothing of value, and there is no more cynical modern spectacle than the seal-clapping, slack-jawed parade of those who did send them jostling to be on camera with their poppies every Remembrance Day. I would suggest that people turn their anger to these awful specimens, rather than focusing on dissenting soldiers.

Soldiers can refuse and soldiers can renege on contracts and soldiers can reject orders. What's more, in the case of Afghanistan, they are entitled to. It's in the rulebook that either a general objection to all wars or a specific objection to a particular war must be examined and heard. If the objection is recognized – which is fairly unlikely as the board for conscientious objectors is, like all such things in the military, a kangaroo court – the objector should be discharged.

My brother died. I had just arrived back in barracks when Clare rang to tell me. He had been strong and ambitious and only twenty-eight. He had been training racehorses in Newmarket. I can only imagine he got a chest infection and tried to shrug it off like so many of us do and went to bed to rest. He never woke up. Septic shock, the coroner told us. He hated confrontation, whereas I had inherited my mother and father's belligerence. He was the gentlest and best of us all. He supported me in my struggle until the day he was suddenly gone. So it goes.

We had a service at the crematorium in York. The racing community is small and tight and many people came. A family friend gave a fine, poetic eulogy about thundering hooves. We held a gathering at York racecourse and I avoided my extended family as much as possible.

I missed a hearing that day. The judge, after being told the reason, complained at my absence. It was the same feeling I got whenever my mother recounted the story of our eviction from my childhood valley again. *It's so hard to get good domestic staff.* The judge's insensitivity, however, was a gift. I got back my rage and bloody-mindedness and disgust. To such people we were nothing.

In the same hearing, the judge went on to question my barrister's professionalism. He suggested that Nick, a life-long campaigner for justice, would bring his political agenda with him and that this should not be allowed. He said this as if the establishment's treatment of objection cases was not consistently political. The judge said, 'I am also aware of Mr Wrack's political position, I think is the word I would use, as secretary of the Respect Party, and it seems to me it would not be right for him to use a case like this in order to make political points.' Nick had never appeared in front of that judge before. He argued in a letter of complaint that the judge was implying that he would use a case in which he had been instructed as a professional barrister to make political points.

This, Nick went on, was 'wholly unacceptable' and 'unjustified' and the judge's comment that he was secretary of the Respect Party was not only 'irrelevant' and 'improper', but 'incorrect'. Nick also enclosed a copy of the document called an 'application for the judge to recuse himself for bias'. To recuse is to step down. The next day, when Nick rang, the judge had retired.

Chapter 13

In October 2009 I added participation in a mass peace demonstration to my rap sheet. My attendance was released to the media about an hour after I left camp on the Friday before the demo. I met Clare in London and, as we sat by the river bracing ourselves with two-for-one mojitos, my troop commander called me. He was a new guy, a paunchy Scot who came across as nervous and was old-looking for a subaltern.

'Do not take part in that demonstration,' he tried to sound authoritative, 'by order of the commanding officer.'

I enjoyed his squirming.

'Do you understand?' he said.

I told him I understood the order perfectly and that I'd see him Monday morning. *Sir.*

I immediately publicized that I was marching in defiance of my CO's orders and we proceeded to Brixton to stay with some friends. I had a suspicion that the army might try and snatch me on the march, and in a way I was hoping for it. That, I knew, would make great television. I had their measure by that time: they craved control and hated transparency and they shrivelled when challenged. That night we drank amounts of red wine far out of proportion with the next day's activities. I guess it was nervousness coupled with the knowledge that I was now in defiance of orders.

Saturday morning, we staggered up to Hyde Park Corner late. I was in no mood to talk so I had a statement read out and stood swaying. Apparently I looked very serious – at least the effects of the mid-range Shiraz were not wasted on the cameras. Having not told the organizers I was hungover, they assumed I was terrified. We set out on the march. It was all whistles and flags and chanting as the column snaked its way to Trafalgar Square, the streets lined with police. The noise was incredible and the atmosphere was raucous. I had never been on a protest march before and it was much more satisfying than running along with a rifle and a bergen.

They didn't snatch me, and that was disappointing, as I had been sure they would. Around twenty thousand marched. I told the crowd that I was a soldier and that I belonged to the profession of arms, and that I could not take part in the war. They roared their approval at me and my decision. I could imagine the hierarchy twitching back at camp.

Back in camp, I got a round of applause from a section of lads as I wandered in on the Monday morning. The troop commander couldn't even look me in the eye, while a section of the seniors laughed at my adventures. One of our ancient corporals said to me, 'Don't let them get to you, Joe, you're only saying what we are all thinking.'

The officer commanding was widely disliked among the troops and I sensed that my activities were not in line with her career plans because she gave me a three-month warning order. Unfortunately for her this was one of the most laughable and toothless disciplinary mechanisms yet created. I struggled to hide my mirth when they went through the list of what I could face: discharge, reprimand, an expression of displeasure or – and here it got really serious – an expression of severe displeasure. I wondered what that would entail. Perhaps it was like an expression of displeasure delivered with a really, really serious face accompanied by a nipple-cripple, Chinese burn or front wedgie carried out in front of the whole regiment on the parade square.

I had never had any disciplinary issues before my AWOL and yet now I was a regular in front of the OC. I was sorry I had never explored it before. I found it filled up the day and provided amusing scenarios for me to recall. From then on I realized the military really was a series of farcical comedy sketches. I was in ascendancy. The brass hated it. The soldiers I worked with loved it. The brass hated this even more.

Around that time the shadow defence secretary attacked me in a right-wing newspaper. It's not entirely true that he attacked me – he was actually using my adventures to score points against his rival in government. He was incredulous with rage, arguing that my actions were 'bad for morale' and that 'nothing seems to have been done to stop him'. This is also not entirely true. Firstly, we should be clear that neither he nor the serving defence secretary had any say over what I did and secondly nothing short of a bullet was going to stop me. Threats, promises of extra time in prison and even expressions of severe displeasure carried no weight with me.

Dr Liam Fox became top dog in defence in the end, eventually getting into cabinet, though only for a while. I know I'm going on a bit, but I take exception to his species questioning my ethics. I watched his later, self-inflicted fall from grace with enormous interest. And at the time it was empowering to know my elected representatives were aware of me. Well, that and my terrible man-crush on this magnificent fellow who appears to be have been roughly as popular as a bar in a mosque.

I had finally been given my appointment with a psychiatric nurse. I had missed my first one due to it being arranged for after the deployment date of my second tour, by which time I was a fugitive. However I maintain I was only ever late once in the army, admittedly by two years. But that's still only once. The nurse was lovely. I felt robbed that I hadn't met her before. She was treating a number of the soldiers from my squadron and within the limits set by the military she did a good job. She even sent me on a day-long course to RAF Brize Norton to talk about anger management to a room full of tense-looking servicemen and women. I had a lot of anger, but I needed it.

My media activity continued but I did not take money, though our sergeant accused me several times of building up a secret fortune. A magazine offered five hundred pounds for an article with Clare. We could not take it so I asked them to give it to a prominent military charity. This was before I recognized that particular crowd and those kinds of things in general as one of the most sordid features of the war industry. These kinds of organizations seem to reflect an effort to stimulate jingoism and the whole operation confused me for a while. I personally believe these initiatives were sparked by increasing opposition to the wars – particularly Afghanistan – as much as by altruism. This kind of pseudo-patriotism had not been so prevalent in the UK when I left. But by the time I got back, the so-called poppy mafia was patrolling like vigilantes. The charities support the government's political line indirectly by encouraging us to simply support the wounded troops regardless of the politics.

Any reasonable person feels for wounded young soldiers, but by trying to strain out the politics, this insidious programme does the job of blurring the line between supporting the wars and supporting the troops. The latter is a meaningless expression in its commonly used sense. The former – supporting the wars – is just nonsense. Neither the government nor its public relations apparatus is stupid enough to request it openly, as in 'support our pointless war'. That these slogans all translate roughly to 'support our foreign policy' is not hard to see. People – good people, no doubt – contribute to these charities much as I contributed. The problem is that people absorb the seemingly apolitical message, which is further lubricated with slick marketing and greasy patronage, but it is not quite so apolitical when you look at the line-up. Among the goblin parade you'll find columnists renowned for rants about race and trades unionists, soldiers turned pundit and establishment favourite, senior oil company executives, royals, judges and generals.

Goodwill is paying for services the government should – and could – be providing, while taxes go into wars with no mandate. All this is done with the approval of the government that has seen the victims wounded and damaged on a set of falsehoods. The returning wounded are then pumped for more precious jingo. There is a whole pumping 'hero' industry pillaging the public for approval as well as the money to clear up the bodies, and the whole racket encourages folk to internalize the lies. If it weren't sickening, the sleight of hand would be admirable.

Many soldiers I served with told me that they didn't want fancy homecomings or flag-draped coffins or anything other than to go quietly home to their families if they were killed or wounded. They didn't want political capital made of them, dead or alive. This was before *and* after the rise of the hero industry. In short, the soldiers and the politics can't be separated. They are not out there trick-or-treating, but doing a purely political job for political ends.

Not long after the defiant demonstration I was arrested at work by two portly military police officers, or monkeys as they are known. I noticed on the paperwork that this was done under an enhanced section of PACE (Police And Criminal Evidence Act), which is used to trim civil liberties and detain peace campaigners and other terrorists. They had decided I was a terrorist so I can only assume they were terrified. A terrorist is someone who takes part in politically motivated violence, yet my public refusal to take part in politically motivated violence saw me arrested as a terrorist. They made me tea and fed me biscuits.

They let me go until Monday when I was dragged into the regimental HQ and told I was being detained under two charges of disobeying standing orders. Standing orders are the permanent, overarching set of orders which, among other things, forbid soldiers to speak to the press without a script. I asked the new adjutant if the charges were those that had been raised following my newspaper and radio interviews, and then withdrawn several weeks earlier. He said they were the very same. I asked if they were the charges that had been withdrawn by a judge in a British court of law and no longer existed. They were. I was being rendered for my political activities.

I was held for a number of days in the camp's detention centre. The cells were freezing and the water ran cold and brown. Nonetheless I caused havoc. I knew the men on guard well enough to be able to push the boundaries of my imprisonment. Once, when my sergeant major – a very small and impeccably uniformed Liverpudlian – was on duty he walked in to find me unguarded, reading the *Independent* and sipping tea behind the reception desk. This pleased me more than it did him. One of the African lance corporals from my squadron was brought in from AWOL. He had been on the run and plucked off a plane bound for Kenya. One morning, as we were unlocked, I heard him shouting as he was ordered to stand to attention for a visiting officer. 'No,' he screamed, 'last night I spoke to God and he told me not to do anything you say.' I felt it unfair that he was getting visits. Outside the cage door separating the cells from the world, there was a small office. On the wall was a long list of absentees from the regiments housed in Dalton Barracks. Since my return I had slipped from the regiment's most wanted position.

I was sent to Colchester military prison after a few days, squeezed into a car between soldiers from my squadron. We smoked on the way down and laughed about the situation. We got to about two-thirds of the way and realized the duty clerk had forgotten the paperwork. Back we went again, and then more fags. I was guarded in a service station by one of the privates. I wandered around just to terrorize him, I kept moving suddenly and they all jumped. Two of them were medically downgraded with lower limb injuries and the other one carried plenty of extra pounds. I reckon I could have outrun them and I thought about escaping, but stilled that idea. One of them was a new kid, wide-eyed and stupid.

'What've you done then, mate?'

I laughed.

'Can't tell you exactly, mate. But I can tell you I am the most dangerous man in the world. That's why they sent *you*.'

He seemed to believe me for a moment. 'Fuck off,' he fell back on the normal squaddie response.

'Here, mate,' I stepped off towards the toilets and they scuttled after me, 'I'm going for a piss. Do you have to hold my cock? Is that in your remit?'

They didn't know what a remit was. They were just kids.

Chapter 14

It was December and I was in prison with Tommy the Hamster, Trevor and Summers. During my time on remand demonstrations were held outside the gates and I received my first few hundred letters. I was an unusual case and well received for it – even some of the screws were supportive. I was entitled to custody hearings once every few weeks to reassess my detention. My first custody hearing – video-linked to the outside world – was presided over by the judge advocate general himself.

The custody reviews, I still suspect, were decided before I pressed the remote on the video-link. When I did press it the JAG and the very acme of the chinless wonder, one Captain Merlin Fitzchinnery-Monguillard of Army Legal Service, appeared on the screen. On one portion of the screen was a pleasant, camp little man who carried out some scribing task during hearings. He'd squealed when Fitzchinnery-Monguillard appeared. *'Merlin is with us!'*

Nick, my barrister, a man of enormous ability and experience, attacked the army for the lack of meaningful charges. The judge asked me if I would speak out again if released. I told him I was obliged to do so. He told me he was sympathetic to my position but that I would not be released unless I stopped. *If you don't speak to the media you can get out.*

I decided I'd stay, given that I had something of an obligation as well as a reputation to uphold by then. Other than that, it was just a case of following the drills as taught to us.

Years ago, on capture, the idea was to give name and rank, number and unit. I recalled being told since, in the training for my second Afghan tour, that upon capture by the enemy one should hold out as long as possible until all operations had been adjusted to your capture. So I would hold out, we would argue our point in the public forum until they broke or they didn't. Any time served on remand would come off the sentence they drummed up later. I didn't work for them anymore, they didn't get a say. They were the enemy, and I had been captured.

I turned down bail. I knew the army was trying to grind me down. I was told that the Military Correctional Training Centre (MCTC) would treat my post-traumatic stress during remand. Needless to say they did not treat me. I was going nowhere. If they'd let me out I'd have carried on and I remain proud of my insolence. I could live with being a prisoner of conscience, although I found the term melodramatic.

I was driven down to London to be assessed by a civilian psychiatrist in a small office in Harley Street. I told him I had been told I had 'low mood' by the army before I went AWOL, and for an hour he questioned me on my symptoms and ripped that diagnosis to shreds. He was astonished that they could have come to that conclusion and diagnosed me with post-traumatic stress, saying he would write his report to that effect and recommended that I receive proper treatment rather than a custodial sentence.

The second hearing followed on with the first having served as something of an intelligence gathering exercise. When the gagging condition was rolled out again, we agreed to it. I figured that by now my position was fairly clear.

The prosecution was devastated: the lead prosecutor had a little lip wobble when the judge released me. It turned out he'd had a whole team of lawyers with him off-screen, such was the army's determination to keep me in prison. Nick had challenged him because he kept turning to mute and talking to people off screen. It is to Nick's credit that he beat the lot of them.

We argued that lack of treatment and isolation were making my condition worse. Our argument was sound and I believe it swayed the JAG personally, but they couldn't accept officially that they were in the wrong. I was given back my civilian clothing and dropped off at the train station. I had been given a train ticket back to Oxford, and off I went. Back at camp the CO, newly returned from Kuwait, called me in and read through the bail conditions again just to make sure. I went home for the weekend and never went back to my unit. I went sick on Monday morning at the army barracks in York and got signed off by a doctor as 'bedded down at home', which is the holy grail of army sick notes. For the moment I had done enough. Besides which, I did not work for them any more.

Chapter 15

We had a tense Christmas in York. I went to Brize Norton for another military psychiatric assessment. The prosecution had ordered one of their own and we expected that they would try to talk down the earlier diagnosis. We were right – the RAF shrink was determined that it was less than PTSD. He didn't know I'd already had one report done, so I let him try his best before slipping in that I'd already been diagnosed. He stopped trying at that point. He told me it might have been down to my drinking, focusing on the symptom rather than the cause. He filed a report saying I had adjustment disorder and possible PTSD, which was in our favour overall. On the way back to York we stayed with Clare's relatives in the Midlands. While carrying logs for their open fire I managed to drop one and it broke my toe. It was a minor problem at the time, but it would come to hinder me later on.

In York I reported to the barracks fortnightly for a reassessment. The civilian doctor there was a kind and kindred spirit. He was campaigning for a proper inquest – in fact, *any inquest* – into the death of Dr David Kelly, the UN weapons inspector who'd died in the woods near his home after shaking up the government's Iraq fictions. The GP explained to me that he had been told by a ranking military psychiatrist that PTSD is underdiagnosed in the military as a matter of course.

The date for my court martial was set for 5 March. As the trial edged closer Nick and his assistant prepared a magnificent defence document and served it on the opposition. It showed that I was guilty of nothing of note. I had been correct to refuse to return to Afghanistan and justified in being AWOL. Further, it was a legal duty to refuse to serve in Afghanistan. I wish I'd been there to see them reading it. It was my intention that my trial be used to indict the government.

By that time, I was facing decades. The draconian new Armed Forces Act had come into force, carrying a potential sentence of ten years per charge. It is a bizarre piece of legislation – soldiers can now be sentenced to ten years for 'failing to escape the enemy'. I later read the journalist and independent MP Martin Bell's memoir, in which he wrote that the whole thing had been rubber-stamped with minimal discussion. He even tried to raise questions about it when he was on the select committee, but his enquiries were turned away and the legislation was pushed through without any thought for the military personnel it would affect.

After a few weeks we decided to see what they had thought about our defence document. I'd never denied being AWOL. I had denied desertion and I'd asserted that I was obliged to speak out. A few hours later my legal team heard back. They'd dropped the lot, except the AWOL. We laughed at the stupidity of it. All those promises of extra time for speaking out, all those interrogations, and they had rolled over. We hadn't even got into the courtroom proper. *Cowards*. In the end I guess they thought better of it. They didn't want to be publicly embarrassed anymore. The admittedly rather toothless Chilcott enquiry into Iraq had been going on at the same time. It was clear they'd dropped the charges to avoid more public examination of the war.

Of course the AWOL was still a serious charge, but the upper ceiling for sentencing is nine months – six with an early guilty plea. Plus, we had my service record, my exceptional disciplinary record, my voluntary return, my PTSD, the bullying and the psychiatrist's recommendation that I shouldn't serve a custodial sentence. A few days later it was announced that on the same day as my plea was to be submitted, Gordon Brown would attend Chilcott. I pled guilty to AWOL. It was a tactical choice as I knew that their guidelines suggested a suspended sentence. It only remained to see what they would do.

A few days before the court martial sentencing in Colchester, the regimental clerk called me and told me to go to court in uniform. I told him I had none and that as I was at home in York I was unable to get one. This was a lie on my part, which I regretted because that clerk had been so supportive. I had just left camp having emptied my room. I had decided I would wear a suit to court.

When we turned up in Colchester, the place was rammed with media. We saw one of the journalists we knew and he asked me what I expected. I told him 'jail'. Two lads from my unit had turned up with my new troop commander to act as escorts. As we passed by, people offered their support. A demo gathered outside the gates and soldiers were beeping their support as they passed. We settled in for the proceedings in a room full of journalists and campaigners. The judge for the case was a recent replacement and with her were four officers. One of the officers was a small man from a Scottish regiment and as they marched in, the hackle (feather) in his hat seemed to be the only thing visible from behind their desk. Another one was a regimental sergeant major from the Dental Corps.

Here I was, I thought, putting my hand up to being involved in war crimes for which they didn't even want to try and find me guilty. They weren't that stupid after all. John, seated beside me, nodded up at them and told me that 'they think God put them up there above everyone, but if you look there are steps'.

The prosecution was an elderly, pristinely uniformed RAF group captain who had nothing to contribute other than reading out the charges. When Nick mentioned the papers he'd prepared it was abundantly clear that the panel and the judge had not actually read them. A gasp went around the courtroom. I suspected the sentence had been decided long before we got there. Even some of the court staff suppressed laughs. The psychiatrist came up to the stand. He told the court he had recommended against a custodial sentence and that I should be treated for my PTSD.

Clearly embarrassed, the judge and her panel read the documents and then Nick launched into his mitigation, which went on for two hours – the longest he'd ever done. As he spoke, I stared the judge and panel down, especially as he read out the passages about bullying, PTSD, harmony guidelines and my objections. The judge squirmed like a scolded head girl, before announcing that they would retire and decide my sentence. Nick had been standing for so long his leg seized up and it nearly gave way underneath him.

We waited tensely in a side room. We took the piss out of my new troop commander, who'd turned up as military escort – she had a camouflage notepad holder. 'What a geek,' I said. 'How keen are you, boss?' My camouflage notepad holder was safe at home, the illicit secret of my keener days, forever ingrained with Afghan and African dust. The wait was awful and I was relieved when we were called back in. The judge, having read the mitigation by now, went into a tirade about duty, bizarrely bringing up the media charges which were no longer there, and thus were to be omitted from the sentencing. It was as if those charges hadn't been with-drawn. They ignored the sentencing guidelines and I was given nine months, of which I would serve four. She claimed to have taken into account my service record, my voluntary return, but the sentence did not tally with the offence. The sentencing guidelines say the starting point for any AWOL is nine months, and then each bit of mitigation takes off weeks or months. The nine-month sentence I received, we later argued, logically meant that the starting point used by the judge and the panel was something like two years.

I took some comfort from the room being full of journal-ists. I thanked the guys who'd helped me while Nick swore to appeal. The young lieutenant and my escorts led me down-stairs. I could hear the shouting outside, a whole crowd of cameramen and protestors had assembled. The officer turned to me, 'Don't speak to the media when we get outside,' she ordered. I walked out, flanked by escorts. A roar went up from the assembled crowd as I thrust a fist up into the air.

From there I was put into the cage of a military police van and driven around to the medical centre. The TA troop com-mander tried to get me to sign documents as we waited. I told her I wasn't going to sign anything and she didn't try again. I was taken to a doctor who assessed me. I told him about my PTSD. He tried to assure me I'd get proper treatment inside, I told him I wouldn't. He had been watching my adventures on television. He shook my hand and wished me good luck.

We ducked out the back way and past my old block to the prison. The screws on duty that day were decent sorts and they remembered me. At MCTC you are meant to march up and halt at the position painted on the floor – facing the guardroom. I decided to sack the marching off and I saun-tered up. They said nothing, they must have expected a bit of attitude. They knew me already.

In the back of the guardroom I sorted out my kit with them and someone came from A Company to get me. I was marched over and given a single cell for the night. Four months to push. I spent the afternoon writing up the day's events for posterity. It felt like coming home would feel if you lived in a dodgy military prison.

Chapter 16

MCTC is nothing more or less than a prison. If you're the parent of a serviceman and your son or daughter is sent there, they are in prison. Don't believe the people with jangling keys and crackling radios who say otherwise. MCTC is flawed, because being both a prison and a military facility, it is fertile ground for extraordinary levels of stupidity. Of the prison's departments, the education centre alone fared better albeit with one serious flaw: the education it provided. Unless you count a day's course on angle-grinding, a non-certificate in plumbing or a day of CV writing as education. It fares better simply because it is a sanctuary for a few hours a day from the snow globe world of A and D companies.

But what really damned the place was its failure to correct, rendering it a poorly administrated borstal for squaddies. The reason for this is that it's already inside a military system which ingrains, compounds and encourages the offences that it punishes. It is a storehouse for naughty soldiers and jaded young men with PTSD. The only reason people don't escape is that there is an automatic two-year sentence for doing so. Nonetheless, people are known to jump the fence and head out for booze and dope.

The main offences are violence, drugs, drink-related offences, fraud, AWOL, theft and desertion. Some of the prisoners, who had previously spent months on remand in civilian prisons before being sentenced, missed civilian prison and were visibly happy to be transferred back to Colchester. Others, however, craved it and wanted to go back and serve their time in civilian nicks: there is less bullshit, no marching, better food, less aggravation from screws, as well as screws who actually know what they are doing, more remission, better facilities and no military uniforms. The only down side, according to these connoisseurs, is that you have more lockup time. 'But', as they say, 'it's fucking prison, innit?' and that kind of thing has to be expected.

There are two types of prisoners here and only one type of gaoler. There are detainees under sentence (DUS) or detainees not under sentence (DNUS). Respectively, these terms mean convicted prisoners and prisoners awaiting trial. They are all crammed into the prison's shabby network of one-storey buildings. The DUS are further subdivided into those who are 'soldiering on' and those who are being discharged. Any sentence under two years brings a convict here, more than two years means civilian prison. Those who are staying in are regarded as unfortunate – they will go through a period of reprogramming in A Company, a second basic training, and they will be messed around for the length of their sentence. Those who are getting out do not give a shit, but seem to have been the better soldiers – the brighter and sharper ones. A Company seems largely reserved for younger soldiers, and D Company is for jaded veterans in their twenties, many of whom had been NCOs failed by the ever-clunking system.

The prisoners are marshalled by screws who are burnt out, promotional failures, wounded, tired of the nomadic life of the field military and people who don't want to die in Afghanistan. 'Fuck that,' a former sergeant from the Guards told me, 'I've got fucking kids, mate. My fucking mate got killed last year … nearly a year to the day.' As a member of the Military Provost Service, there are few tours and very little to do on them except possibly open a hatch and peer in at a captured insurgent every hour or so. Naturally, these screws, who have never been locked up in a civilian prison, tell us this is much better. 'Look,' they tell us, 'you get all this retraining, you get all this good food, you get us helping you all the time, you get to polish boots, you get to use the education centre – did you know you can learn how to use an angle grinder here?' Set you up for fucking life, that.

By then I knew prison well enough to handle it, but that first night was hardest.

I was alone and locked in a single cell. I was refused a shower or food, but I had tobacco. Smoking and thinking, I looked around my cell and saw the sheet of paper taped to the door at chest height. It listed everything in the room, chair, bed, soldier box. What the fuck was a soldier box? I scanned the cell and noted the square wooden footlocker under the bed. These lockers are painted grey and cut with generous air holes for when high-spirited soldiers occasionally tried to stuff each other inside them. I'd seen a hundred of them in my career but I'd never known what they were called. For a moment I'd thought it meant the cell itself, as in a box to put soldiers in. Like the rubbish they spout about the army, the myth. The box, the ideological compartment in which the military existed, was made out doctrine and ideas, myths and fantasies about soldiers. I would never be in that box again; I had fought my way out.

One of the A Company had approached me the next day and told me not to talk 'poll-o-ticks' to the other new inmates as some of them were staying in the army. He chewed the word around his mouth. Apparently, he took me for a mutineer of some kind, which showed him to be fairly astute. I told him I didn't talk 'poll-o-ticks' unless asked and he left it at that. He was so keen that he would often assemble us all on impromptu parades and give us shit for transgressions which were unknown to us. We prisoners would stand there exchanging looks. 'Right! Any questions?' Then, even as hands went up he would spin on his heel and march away with a panache and assurance entirely at odds with his communication skills. He was a permanent emergency. He was a keen one, but some of the other turnkeys were just faces seeing out their time. Later on that day, I was told that I would see the commanding officer the next day for my first interview.

'You're that bloke who did that thing!' An accusatory voice rang out as I was dumping my kit on an empty bed in my new room in D Company. I hate being on display. He was a kid, he looked about ten.

'Yeah, mate,' I told him.

'You're a fucking legend, can't wait to tell my mum I'm in here with a celebrity!' he said and scampered off.

The atmosphere in D Company was always somewhere between carnival and insurrection. No one gave a care anymore: troops milled around the rooms smoking the thinnest rollups ever, gathering here and there. People helped themselves to brews from the stained urn that was put out mid-morning and mid-afternoon. The tea was brown and warm and tasted of nothing. We called it coff-tea and people loaded it with sugar from an ancient ice-cream container while we elbowed for biscuits.

I'd moved into D Company from A Company after my meeting with the commanding officer that morning. He was an energetic, eccentric man who reminded me of Professor Weeto from the cereal packet. He was benevolent enough that day to spare me the bullshit of A Company, despite the army dragging their feet over my discharge. In theory, I was meant to stay in A Company because I had not been discharged at my sentencing. The judge either forgot or didn't do it for some reason I could not fathom. They were unlikely to convince me to 'soldier on'. I was told to wheel my stuff on a handcart down the long corridor – from the well-buffed and soldierly floors of A Company to the dull, scuffed and insolent floors of D Company.

As time went on, I began to see that the men in D Company tended not to give a fuck in a real, true and collective manner. They didn't polish their boots unless they had to, contraband was everywhere, prisoners challenged the screws and did the very minimum to get their weekly 'scores' and earn remission. Often, they didn't even do that. Every corps, regiment and service of the British military seemed to be represented here. With a few exceptions, the airmen and sailors were there for fraud and the soldiers were there for the other crimes.

Both A and D Company prisoners were organized according to a point-based staging system which the screws reinterpreted as they saw fit, denying people progression at times and at others just forgetting who people were and mixing up reports. Advancement was based on time served, behaviour, turnout, and so on. If you played the good lad you might move up more quickly. I'd heard of people being offered quick advancement for grassing or reporting on fellow prisoners. To my knowledge these were most often turned down flat. Prisoners hated the screws more than they annoyed each other. Generally people tried to strike a balance between getting through the staging system and winding up the turnkeys as much as possible. It was guerrilla warfare. There seemed to be a kind of unspoken pact that if we were all fairly rubbish, then mediocre started to look impressive.

Nobody wanted to be branded as a sycophant to the screws – it just wasn't worth it.

In stage one you wore a black and green badge on your uniform. Stages ones were 'locked down' in their rooms in the evenings, at night and for an hour or so after lunch. Every morning there were inspections: lockers had to be laid out in a certain way, beds made, best boots polished (we had a working, day-to-day pair and a pair just to display on inspections) and you had to come to attention and make a little statement when the screw got to you. For example, you might have to say, 'Staff, I am 748 DUS Glenton, currently in week four, sentenced to nine months, currently employed on induction week, staff.' It was like basic training. Each week, if you scored enough you got a 'recommend' and four or five of these moved you up the staging system. I got a guardsman to polish my boots and never touched them again during my sentence. My polishing days had ended.

In stage two you were moved to an area off limits to the stage ones. You weren't locked down as often and were given a new green and red tag to mark you out. Inspections were easier, with lockers only inspected two mornings a week. There was a ping-pong table and we got very good at playing. Stage two also contained the stage two-and-a-halves. These prisoners wore red and blue tags on their chests, had permission to move around camp on their own during the day and got more money to spend on tobacco and sweets. They were waiting to get to stage three where they would be given separate accommodation at the back of the prison and were never locked down, suffered few and less rigorous inspections and got day release on Saturdays with thirty pounds in actual cash to spend.

People moved down the system as well as up. When I arrived in stage one, I was joined by a group who had just been busted down to the lowest stage, which was called one bravo. Little Scouse and Big Scouse were from a Rifles regiment and were superb barrack-room lawyers. Those two spent a lot of time in the gym and, until their demotion, had smuggled in protein powder to help them get big, and drugs to pass the rest of the time. They'd bought Vodka in town, left it against the back fence near the stage three accommodation, and then they nipped out and squeezed it through the chain links. They got shit-faced and Big Scouse battered one of their cellmates. They'd just emerged from the punishment block where they'd been trussed up in isolation in cold cells with no possessions, no contact and no visits. They didn't mind – they had more time than me still left to serve and would reach stage three again before they were released.

The room was built for eight convicts but accommodated only six with my arrival. There was a twenty-one-year old infantryman named Tobacco, a kid who looked about fourteen called Timmy, another infantryman named Sharp, a Nigerian kid from the Rifles, a young Welshman and me. They were a mix of AWOLs, drugs and one glassing. Tobacco was so named because he had contraband and he proved generous. His battalion, he told us, liked steroids. While he'd been on leave the accommodation was raided and the collected steroids had been stashed amongst his kit. He was still being investigated and was on edge waiting for a charge sheet. His regiment couldn't have been too bothered because two days before his discharge they dropped the outstanding charges and took him back.

At the start I befriended Sharp more than the others. He was a quiet kid from London and the adopted son of evangelists. He had a photo of a pretty Kenyan girl on his locker. A Kenyan colleague from his German-based regiment had decided that their affair was racially inappropriate and gone for him one night in a club. Sharp had a drink in his hand and bottled him, panic hitting. They dropped attempted murder in the end and he got eighteen months for GBH. His main concern was acquiring weed and smoking the sharp edge off his woes. That was unlikely – at least in stage one. They were decent men and if you went by their stories you'd never find a higher concentration of innocent men. Except me – the guiltiest of the horrible lot by a stretch and proudly so.

The staff in D Company ranged from poor to poorer with a sprinkling of decent types. They didn't know how to deal with me. Some were sympathetic, others were worried I'd out them if they fucked up. One or two were quite human. One of these was a Military Cross winner from an infantry regiment. He was on temporary loan and hated the regime as much as we did. He had been interred here only a year before and had been busted down to private. But every time he fucked up, normally drink-related, he'd go back to his commanding officer and get his rank back. He was too good at soldiering to lose. He'd slain a bunch of insurgents in Iraq after they'd ambushed some dignitary his unit had been escorting. He had killed them with their own weapons for good measure.

He'd also been in Afghanistan when I'd been there, only he had been stuck on a hill for over a hundred days getting mortared. Apparently it was the longest static trench defence in British army history. A deal was cut with the Taliban and the insurgents had actually picked up the Ulstermen in trucks, driven them out and dropped them off four miles from base. The Taliban, he told us, had left them to walk the rest of the way. He was here because some shrapnel in his body had left him temporarily exempt from operations. He was always friendly towards us all, giving us smokes and telling us his tales. He crazed the regimental sergeant major by talking to us like people. 'Fokkit,' he'd say in his impenetrable Belfast accent, 'they can kick me out. I'll go back to my regiment, no bother.'

He also told us how he felt about his medal, and more specifically about his citation. He said he was on watch keeping duty one night and found his citation – the little report to recommend a medal – being used as a template for others. This he put down to a culture he called 'morale medals': the awarding of medals for publicity purposes.

On arrival in D Company there was another week of induction training. This included a day of writing CVs and a day of 'citizenship' training. We were also expected to debate some political issues and one sergeant promised me my soapbox. He seemed to believe I was particularly intelligent and worthy of respect. We discussed immigration and soon a casual racism emerged, with a number of the group expounding the values of the BNP. They said this was because that group represented really British things that had been diluted with the coming of brown people and their foreign ways. I argued that just because the BNP might offer, for example, to change your granny's wheelie bins twice a week instead of once, they remained fascists. I told them that much of the jingoistic stuff they talked about was rubbish and was derived from a shaky view of history. Some of the lads talked about the dubious merits of Churchill or a mythical, golden British Empire. I told them this was all very contradictory.

Next we were required to find positives and negatives from the premiership of Tony Blair. My positive was that he was no longer in office; among my negatives was that he had been. Iraq, one sergeant argued, was now a better place. I told him that anything up to a million people could not agree or disagree with him because they had been murdered there. There was a suggestion that it was not us, but the Americans who had done this and I explained that the accessory is an offender as well as the criminal. Our debate ended on bruised myths and the knowledge that I had become very political and conscious and that my arguments were better than theirs.

They accepted ideas from on high, much as they accepted the fiction that MCTC was about correction. The screws, at least, were utterly convinced that the prison in which we stood was not a prison. They were sure of this, even when you pointed out the HMP (her majesty's prisons) legislation, or the panic that ensued when I had would overhear HMP calling a day early to warn of a 'snap' inspection, or what it said in the 'statutory instrument' documents. This legislative rulebook for the facility, which I risked privileges to smuggle in, explained that prisoners, guards and governor are merely to be renamed 'detainees', 'staff' and 'commandant' while retaining the same roles and powers.

Chapter 17

A month or so into my sentence, my appeal took place at the
Royal Courts of Justice in London. My heart sank straight
away when I heard they had assigned the lord chief justice
himself to preside. The name alone was an indicator that he
had been custom-bred for dealing with rabble-rousers. Two
soldiers from my regiment had been dispatched in the early
hours to pick me up. A corporal from my squadron was in
charge of the detail and complained loudly while the driver
managed to get us lost for an hour in London. He told me
he planned to let me go if they freed me and play ignorant
when he got back to camp. He couldn't be arsed driving
back to Colchester, as this would have caused problems for
the prison: an unprocessed parolee wandering around newspaper offices and television studios. If only for that, I prayed
for release.

Whatever happened, it was to be a day in the sun for me.
There was a crowd of protestors outside the courts and as
I looked up at the magnificent building I couldn't help but
wonder how much it cost. We went in and waited in the café
which was full of pinstriped legal types and assorted toffs.
Nick told me that we were going to play it on the basis of
time already served and the mitigating factors that had
been ignored.

Nick wanted to appeal what we considered was the fatuous nature of some of the court martial's findings. The judge had claimed that my absence had been at a critical point and that the army had been forced to deploy someone else in my place. Not a single piece of evidence was put before the court to support this claim. You would think judges would be sticklers for that kind of thing. Even if I hadn't known that this was untrue, even if the young soldiers who had gone on that tour hadn't told me themselves that when they did eventually deploy people some were pulled off the plane as it waited to take off for Afghanistan.

But we went into the appeal with no illusions. By allowing the appeal I believed they were trying to give the whole debacle an edge of legitimacy. Especially after a court martial that had looked, from where I was sitting, like a bona fide kangaroo court. It had been passed straight to this lord chief justice character – the second highest judge in the land. I considered complaining that I did not have the highest. We sat outside and chatted in the sun, before drifting back through the cool, vaulted passages to our hearing.

The prosecution was a brigadier and he let us get on with it. Nick laid down the case for mitigation. When the judges came out and started to deliver their verdict it looked good. Spirits were high and the corporal kept getting deadly looks from the typist for taking the mick out of the judges so loudly. They threw the appeal out in the end, arguing that the court martial was a 'specialist' court and they were unwilling to go against its findings. As judges they made sure to drag it out and use ten words wherever two would have done. The result made us wonder why, if that was the case, they had even bothered. That decision could've been made without disturbing my gym and reading time in prison. Poor Nick had spent all that time building up a case and never really got to wield it, but the research is all there ready for the next guy. Cowards, I thought. It had been a non-event in legal terms. I gave the cameras a wave as we left.

I got a lot of mail in prison. I kept the letters, thousands of them – ten or twenty letters in a day, once it was two hundred. I also received gifts: an Easter egg, money, flowers. The mail crazed the screws because they had to open every one, except when they got lazy. Then, if their superiors were not around, they would let me do it. Their aggravation made getting mail doubly pleasing. Thousands of miles from the site of that plane crash near Kandahar, I received a letter from the bereaved father of an airman who had died on that flight. He quoted Wellington to the effect that the true test of a general is to know when to retreat and to have the courage to do it.

Of all of these letters, coming from all over the world – Russia, Brazil, Australia, Europe, America – only one was negative. Had I expected an easy ride? With respect to my air force comrades the letter was marked RAF, and at the time I laughed. It repeated the same tired stuff: contract, queen's shilling, honour, dishonour and similar moralistic bullshit. No newer or better arguments against my refusal emerged from it. I gave this one a proud position on the top of a stack of others just to balance the debate. One of my cellmates was enraged by this letter and wrote a response which I told him not to send.

Another letter was from a man named Hubert Lewis – late of the RAF. He wrote thinly on yellowed paper to tell me he had been in a bomber crew in the war. He wrote to me saying that if he did not protest my incarceration, he and his mates would have fought for nothing. It was truly powerful and I hoped I would get to meet him when I got out.

I received a letter from a peace group who had put my name forward for a peace prize. It was called the Hrant Dink Award. Hrant Dink was a Turkish-Armenian journalist murdered for his activism. Although I did not win the award – I may not even have been considered – I presented the letter nominating me to the prison staff and it strained them. The official line was that I was in no way a political prisoner of any kind so this situation blazed out their circuitry. As they did not know what to say, they stared at the letter as I held it through their little hatch, then at me, then at each other. It was above their pay scale. The lady in the education centre who was kind, helpful and civilian thought it was good that I'd been put forward.

In D Company rebellion was only ever moments away. Once, while I sat alone in my room, the most vocal, robust clique of prisoners filed in. They had a punchy air and I thought that they wanted to fight. They did, but not with me. They had decided I was a rebel of note and they wanted advice on fighting the regime. The media, I told them, is always the way. But it must be done anonymously. We plotted behind closed doors for a long time – sit-downs, letters, sabotage, disobedience. These men were angry and vengeful. Taken with their spirit, I got in touch with people on the outside. I related back to them that rebellion carried a potential ten-year sentence for mutiny in the prisons. Most of us were on short sentences so we weighed it and left it. My revenge, and I hope a little of theirs, exists in this book. Two of the lessons I had learned were clear to me then: the sunlight makes their slime dry up, and you must only fight when you can win something or bloody the opposition.

Nonetheless, other prisoners took up the cause to 'Free Joe Glenton'. By then there was a T-shirt available and they took the slogan from the advertisement for it, which I had printed out and stuck on my locker door. In jest, I wrote on the paper that you could buy them for half price with an army ID card. The chanting was not really about me, but it pissed the screws off so the prisoners felt they had to do it. They chanted it on parade and the gaolers would shout and complain. Big Scouse and Little Scouse liked the idea a lot. They took it further and danced on parade, affecting rich African accents and singing 'Free Nelson Mandela'. The screws responded by saying that I could not be a political prisoner because MCTC was not a prison. They had convinced themselves of this, much as I once convinced myself of the deep rightness of the war. Like them, I was wrong.

I did not just have agreement inside, I also had visits from outside the prison. One day, as I was sitting in the reception area waiting for a legal visit, John came marching towards me flanked by my old lawyer. The guy I had sacked was unaware of who John was and chatted to him as they walked to the visiting hall. Seeing me through the glass as they approached, he made a comment about me being 'a little shit'. John, having overheard the man's name at the guardhouse, knew perfectly well he was the reject from months before. He stopped suddenly, faced the lawyer and got nose to nose as he does to comrades and foes alike, 'Well,' he said and left a long pause, 'I think he's a FUCKING HERO.' The lawyer's eyes went from five pence size to fifty pence size. John's warlike expressions can strip paint. His victim scampered into the visiting hall, relieved as the screws unlocked the doors.

The legal visits punctuated my sentence and were always good. John was a great speaker and excellent for morale. He told me about his travels in the merchant navy, his spell as a boy soldier and when he had been charged with incitement to riot over the Poll Tax. A brawl had broken out in the court, he told me, between the coppers who were testifying and the defendants. John was the most militant person I had yet met and he spoke about familiar ideas – class, freedom, politics, justice, rebellion – in new ways.

Chapter 18

Our sergeant major and officer commanding formed an odd pair. The OC was a navy lieutenant, equivalent to an army captain. He was a limp, scruffy man with a tragic, Amish kind of beard and a vague northern twang, which would sharpen unbidden. He reminded us of a kind of adolescent goth who'd taken to wearing combat uniform. To us he was visibly and unforgivably naval and uncomfortable around soldiers. The lads despised him for his routine condescension, and given an opportunity would have skinned him. As is sometimes the case, the senior NCO in the company was his wet nurse and his sycophant and protected him from the population – we speculated that perhaps the sergeant major bathed the OC and dutifully brought him milk when he was stressed by all us cads and bounders. We have no evidence of this, but the idea pleased us.

The sergeant major was an Irishman, one eye staring off glassily into the middle-distance and with his black, slick, side-parted hair he looked like a Spandau Ballet reject. By some quirk or failure of memory I cannot fully recall him as other than an Irish cyclops – not fearsome but oafish, more bureaucrat then soldier. We duped him regularly and when we were assembled, the Scouse rebels would challenge him from the ranks. He strutted around repeating himself over and over, waving his pace stick. I'd had some good sergeant majors and some poor ones. The issue was never that they enforced discipline – soldiers generally accept that is what any sergeant major does – it goes with the job, like the stick. But this guy loved it. He wasn't in a proper unit for a reason. Men like that are the first to be stitched up by their soldiers who reject their overbearing manner and their self-obsession. He was occasionally friendly but mostly an arsehole. He'd come from A Company and had designs on sorting out D Company. We had other ideas: there would be no shine on D's floors or bulled boots or toeing the line.

I sensed there would be some test before things settled – it came not long after. I had requested books to be brought in, having explained I was going to university and that I wanted to study. This simple request was repeatedly refused, ignored or forgotten even though the books were waiting a few hundred metres away in the visitor's centre. I got onto my lawyer and told him I was being refused my books repeatedly and the library was limited. He rang them up and tore strips off them. Within an hour my books were released and I was marched over to retrieve them.

The chain of command was something to be circumvented. 'Glenton!' growled the staff sergeant on duty as I returned – he was a hulking ex-guardsman, 'We're not here at your beck and call, you know.' I understood perfectly, I explained, my arms straining with books. I should have known there'd be a backlash, maybe it was the assault on their sense of authority or maybe they just didn't rate Trotsky – in places I find him slightly wordy myself, but for a showcase in crisp polemics, I think the turnkeys were cheating themselves.

When they had failed to get me with the books they tried another tack. I was still wearing trainers at this point, having broken my toe. I was sure I'd had a chit for it in among the rolling ones I'd received while on sick leave, but it turned out I didn't. Nonetheless, I'd gone unchallenged about the trainers for weeks. Not least because better than having a piece of paper to prove I had a broken toe, I had an actual broken toe. But as the army saying goes, 'no chitty, no pity'.

One day, as we assembled in a squad to leave the education centre, the quartermaster warrant officer emerged from her stores, wielding her inevitable pace stick. This was her ritual. Five feet tall and broad and ten years past a soldierly exertion, she would often come out just before the end of the day, as we were being marched back for evening meal, and she revelled in her power in the most visible way.

'Where's your belt?' she demanded of someone whose combat jacket hung loose.

'And you, where's your beret?'

'Ain't got one, ma'am,' came the answer.

Her eyes flickered with glee, 'Not good enough. Come to the stores tomorrow and get a jungle hat.'

Her eyes fell upon me and then my trainers. Her palm flicked up towards me, expecting a chit, hoping there wasn't one.

'I think I've got one back in the lines, ma'am,' I said.

She narrowed her eyes and embarked on some drivel about it being no good there. She said something about ringing the lines and scrawled my name in her notepad. She was going to check up on me. The sergeant who'd come to march us back swung open the barred gate and marched us off, everyone pouring scorn on the quartermaster as we went. The sergeant griped at our noise all the way and mumbled to himself as we were checked back in.

We returned to the lines and as I got back to my room, dropping my books off before scoff, the Irishman, came in. 'You'd better find that chit, Joey, the RQMS just called,' he said. I nodded and checked through my locker. It was nowhere to be found.

The oafish sergeant stormed in. 'Glenton,' he ordered sharply, wagging a finger, 'Follow me.'

I followed him, imagining some routine paperwork or a minor bollocking for its own sake. He marched me straight past the company lines and into the long corridor.

'Where are we going, staff?' I asked.

He chortled to himself, 'You'll see.'

I was marched straight into the company sergeant major's office. The screw closed the door behind me.

'My staff,' the CSM drawled, indicating the sergeant (and this was helpful because you could never tell quite where he was looking), 'tells me you just verbally abused the RQMS.' He sat back, looking happy with himself.

I frowned at him, 'Sir, I only said I had a chit in my locker and a broken toe. She asked me about my trainers.'

'No, he informed me that on the way back from the education centre, you abused her.' He looked down at a report, evidently filled out in the last three and half minutes. 'This is unacceptable,' he turned the report around and lifted it to show me.

It clicked: a stitch-up. 'No, I didn't. I didn't say anything at all.' I turned to face my accuser, who was smirking to my left. I met his gaze. 'He is mistaken or he's lying. There were a bunch of other lads there, go and ask them.'

Both their faces dropped.

'Why would I lie?' The screw looked pleadingly at his boss, and came out with the timeless excuse of military perjurers, 'I'm a sergeant and I've been in the army twenty years.'

I wouldn't shout about that, I thought. Being a sergeant after twenty years is pretty fucking poor, especially when you have to work in prison to get that third stripe on your chest. They give them away free in the Turnkey Corps. I bit my tongue.

The CSM looked at his man, unsure – worse, visibly unsure. Then he remembered I was there and told me to wait outside. I heard them chattering frantically before they called me back in.

'My sergeant is sure. He's a member of my staff and I trust him. You will be reduced to one bravo. You may appeal to the OC.'

Seen off, ranks closed.

'He's lying,' I explained, wanting badly to chin the big dumb fuck as he stood there with his smirk back on. 'I'll take the appeal, sir.'

One bravo meant loss of remission and recommend, and the addition of the much talked about itchies and scratchies (old army blankets). One guy had already caught lice from them. I was marched out and returned to D Company lines.

I was brought before the OC. He told me he didn't need reasonable doubt, only balance of probability, and that his men were never wrong. It is impressive to never be wrong – I had never come across that phenomenon before and frankly I didn't fully believe him. I laughed at him and asked if I was being attacked because I was a political prisoner.

He nearly fell of his chair, 'You are not a political prisoner, you are here for AWOL.'

I shook my head, 'I'm here because I attacked the establishment and they threw their own rulebook out.'

We went at it, the officer and the convict, and over ten minutes I levelled his arguments.

He eventually managed to spear himself on a superb line, 'Listen, I know what I'm talking about because I've done, like, a really long course that, like, lawyers and judges and *stuff* do and I am always right, 99 per cent of the time.'

At this, I laughed. Flustered, he continued, 'Get out Glenton – you're boring me.'

An hour later, he called me back in and told me he had asked the witnesses, though by that time I had done the same. All the lads had confirmed I hadn't said anything. But the sergeant was sure, so I would be reduced and forced to wear boots despite my broken toe. I laughed out loud. It was a face-saving exercise. I was busted down, given the old blankets and forced to wear boots. The blankets were never cleaned. I confirmed this when I was issued them, incidentally by my accuser. 'Man up,' he told me.

The next day there were allegations of torture in the media. The hierarchy was flapping, much to my amusement. I refused to use the blankets and one of the lads loyally offered me his duvet. The fortnightly protestors who gathered at the gates now wore blankets and carried a bed sheet with 'End Blanket Punishment' written on it. A decent screw complained to me that they had locked down the whole camp. He told me that a number of the placards outside read 'Troops Go Home', and the presence of the protestors had stopped him doing exactly that. The protests reached right into the prison that week and affected its running, and the OC and CO kept their distance afterwards. The chanting drifted over the walls and freed me for a while.

Chapter 19

Emitting animal noises on parade amused us more than our captors. At least ten times a day the hundred or so prisoners in D Company would gather in the long hall outside the company lines. Three ranks deep, our names would be called and we would come to attention and say 'staff'. If it was a diets (meal) parade, we would then be right-turned and the front rank would lead off – whether we went marching or strolling was mood dependent.

Massive, a brawny Geordie had discovered his chicken noise surpassed any animal noise the rest of us could make. He would add it to the sheep noises which went with human herding. The staff shouted at us when someone started the bleating and would go to where the noise came from. We were clever sheep. Someone would bleat at the other end and the screw would go there, demanding the culprit's identity. From somewhere else a muffled baa would come. Then, as the screws became angrier, more species would be mimicked. We could do cats, dogs, cows and less distinct things. The staff would threaten to keep us there until it stopped. We knew this was a lie. They had their schedules to keep to and we were hurrying nowhere – we were in prison. We would quieten down to lull them. As they right-turned us to march to diets, Massive's chicken noise would echo through the whole prison. They never caught him.

At this time my lack of treatment for PTSD was also leaked to the press. The evidence suggested the way forward: name and shame. The military couldn't really complain about using the media as a weapon. At long last, an appointment appeared. I asked the nurse if she thought prison was conducive to treatment. She told me that the room we were in certainly was. I looked around: it had bars on the windows. She explained that it was an appropriate environment for treatment because it had comfortable furniture. I wondered whether perhaps all my woes could have been avoided by a trip to Ikea. She took me through a session. This involved me focusing on my trauma while she waved her finger in front of my eyes. It smacked of bullshit to me, but I'm no shrink. Some people say it worked for them. Personally, I call it the magic finger.

At stage two and a half I became the prison librarian. This fulfilled a lifelong ambition but my dreams were shattered when I realized there was no trolley to push from cell to cell and none of the books were hollowed out. Now I was allowed to move about camp and I had a chit to say as much, and so I would go early to the library and open it up. Our most widely read section was true crime, followed by some very weak texts on physical fitness. Every day papers were delivered and I deconstructed them – the *Times*, the *Mail*, and so on. I read and wrote between playing librarian, taking fag breaks and drinking coff-tea from the urn in the yard outside.

The smartly turned out lads from A Company came in daily and picked up war books. One of them was from the Household Cavalry and when he realized who I was, he said with a start, 'You're that bloke who did that thing!' I told him I was that bloke who did the protest. He said he had a revelation bubbling: 'I was on duty in London that day. They rang up my guardroom and told us to arrest you. They said there's a soldier about to march and we should take him.'

But they had not taken me. This revelation was bittersweet for me – the photos would have been superb. Besides, on that day, Nelson's column had been tightly surrounded with protestors many ranks deep to stop any policemen.

He carried on, 'Our duty warrant officer told them if they wanted you arrested, they could do it themselves. He told us that he agreed with you.' He paused for a moment. 'We all agreed with you'.

What a fine man this warrant officer had been.

An organization of born-again Christians named the Alpha Course had somehow managed to infiltrate the military. Members gave lectures and so on as part of a recruiting drive and they even had a foothold in prison. It happened on a Sunday and you would be plied with cakes while some botherer strummed and sang about Jesus. Sometimes, for extra flavour, there would be young women, creamy and cake-like and painted up to drag the sinners in. Clearly, the general of the padres or some such had pulled some strings. I have no particular problem with faith, except when the audience is virtually captive and composed of vulnerable young people – which, for all their front and machismo, was what the lads in prison were.

Although attendance was optional, the cakes and the presence of women were nectar for young, vulnerable, often damaged boys. I never knew how the religious group managed to get a beachhead in prison, but I found it all a bit devious and, for me, prison was no reason to abandon reason.

There was a fine and kind woman in the education centre. When we were briefed on the education facilities I asked her if I could study, telling her I was going to university. This pleased her and I suppose it was unusual. I wrote my first ever essay for her. It was on the causes of the First World War. She gave me history books to read – not least, Eric Hobsbawm – and taught me how to cite and reference. I argued that the war was the result of a failure of statesmanship, though I would argue differently now. I was given a room, resources and access to the internet. I read, studied and wrote. I ploughed through *Papillon* in prison and was inspired by the story of bloody-minded, individual resistance and the character's defiance and determination. The prison was almost monastic in those hours.

We all spent a lot of time in the gym. Some would go in and lift weights while staring in the mirror, while others would run for the hour. We had a set of submariners who got skinny over the course of their sentences after so long eating biscuits deep underwater. I hit the bag and the pads. I rediscovered my love of throwing punches and kicks and it helped to while away the days. A few of us started sparring but got stopped by a member of the gym staff. The Scousers were on a personal training course and they showed me how to do compound lifts that were also good for taking up your time. Prison ended up being somewhere between a gulag and a health spa.

In stage three we were left alone for the most part, hidden away in a separate wing of the prison. We had easy inspections, day-release on Saturdays and were first up to eat. Drugs were fairly prevalent and easy to get in there, though I avoided them. Fortunately the screws were clueless about drugs, even if their use was flaunted. The Scouse rebels, a few other lads and I had witnessed this in the exercise yard: the sun was high and the weed smokers had crafted a joint that stunk out the whole area. A screw emerged and came over. He chatted to us for ten minutes as the weed smoke spiralled around him. Not a word, not even a hint of recognition.

People were getting so high that it couldn't go unnoticed any more. Some lads were doing coke and MDMA in their rooms, people were stumbling around giggling and glassy-eyed, their uniform collars dusted with powder. The sergeant major looked physically aroused one day as he strode into stage three accommodation with sniffer dogs and HMP screws in order to rip all our lockers apart. They couldn't find shit, except illicit stashes of chocolate bars. They took us out to the yard and lined us up. A dog was guided around us until it selected a Welsh kid from my corps by sitting next to him. They marched him away to solitary confinement, chuffed with their catch. On interrogation he played innocent and got away with it, though we all – screws and prisoners – knew he was guilty. He revealed to us later that the sergeant major even tried to convince him to be a grass.

Around that time I received a final career report. What moment of brilliance. It told me that I would not be getting promoted that year, which stung me, but I got a wry high score for my communication ability. Presumably this nod was for my efforts as a military media pundit, albeit an illegal one.

Days after the report, I was summoned by the commanding officer for a final meeting before my sentence was done. The charges for speaking to the media had apparently been 'hanging around' in the system. He told me that despite the army being 'confident of a conviction' they had chosen to drop these. I found this claim hilarious as they'd already dropped those charges, reasserted them and dropped them again. So, despite their 'confidence', he drivelled, the army had decided that they could not justify using the public purse to carry them through. It was the MOD's final cop out. I had been willing to incur those charges, to taunt the army and to face the years in prison, which could have been added to my sentence, but they were unwilling to play the game. It was yet another validation of my position. There was a sense of finality to it all.

My release crept closer and I grew restless as time slowed noticeably. The staff stayed out of my way, fearing anything they did was going to be publicly dissected. They even started to be quite nice in their way. A screw tried to convince me that the prison was badly run due to funding issues, but a lack of funding doesn't turn people into arseholes. That's a lifestyle choice. I was supposed to be out on the fourth of July, but their fibs about verbally abusing the quartermaster reduced my remission. The sport had run out by then and so I saved up my ire for bigger fish – bigger than her, or the OC or the CO. My fight hadn't ever been with those little people, but with the almost exclusively old, white, dull, rich, male people who sent us to do things for them – to lubricate their ambitions with our blood. All my anger was being saved up for them.

I was released on 12 July 2010. I took my uniform off for the last time and felt a little bit of sadness. I was leaving the people and that strange military world I had come to know. The feeling didn't linger as two screws marched me out to the gate, and then just before ten that morning they set me free. As we loaded my bags into a car and I prepared to walk down the long drive to where demonstrators and the media were waiting, the OC drove past. He peered out and I thought about the great violence I had wished upon him.

Turning to walk down the long drive, I saw the protestors and newsmen grouped there. As we drew closer, they became framed by my old block at 13 Regiment. Beyond the old block and the journalists and activists was the world beyond all the different Soldier Boxes I had lived in. The real world had cheers to greet me. I was not allowed to speak to the media until after twelve that night as I was still under prison rules. Naturally, I ignored those rules and gave the interviews. I didn't work for the army anymore. I hadn't for some time.

Chapter 20

I left prison and the army on the same day. I will give the government and the army their dues. If the aim was correction then it worked, though not in the intended way, as I emerged from their cage committed to unseating them. Had it been, as they'd promised, many years in prison then I still would have been right to do what I did for every minute of that time served. From the moment I went into jail to the moment I emerged. I truly believe that, and I am grateful for what I learned.

When I got home I compared my grandfather's medals to my own, and turned them both to look at their edges. They were both for Private Glenton, although my army number was much longer than his and they were issued nearly a century apart, but the engraved font was the same.

I researched him for an article much later, to compare our experiences. He had fought at the Piave River in northern Italy. The 28th Division had been sent from the mud of northern Europe to shore up the Italian army. In an imperial land grab deep into Austro-Hungarian territory – now Slovenia – the Italians had gone as far as Caporetto and come unstuck. They had fallen back in disarray.

It was an era of huge dissent, industrial militancy and mutiny. A badly thought out adventure too far from home.

The aristocratic officers of the time – who would later populate the far right under Mussolini – had reintroduced the Roman tradition of decimation. One of these aristocrats said that war was 'hygiene' and they executed soldiers until the rest of their men did what they were told.

Private George Glenton won his military medal there, in his teens. Ernest Hemingway served only miles away and wrote, 'the things which were glorious had no glory'. This also rings true of the War on Terror. George came back a damaged man, as far as we know from family anecdotes. I handed both of our medals to my youngest cousin in case he should ever get ideas about wars and soldiers. Nearly a century had passed between the two sets of fictions told to two different Private Glentons and between the inscription of two sets of lies in two different bits of tin.

While I was in prison my ex-soldier friend had come over from Australia to get married. Clare and my mother went to the wedding. He was upset I had not told him and was very strange throughout the day. Later, after prison, we began to chat again. He was doing a distance university course and we chatted politics by email for a while. Apparently, he had drifted more and more towards the justifications for wars he had once criticized. I thought we could debate the issues. I thought distance learners lost out on actual debate. I dealt with the malformed arguments he threw at me, but they told me a lot: attack Iran, attack North Korea, attack everyone, pro-nuke, pro-market and anti-reason. These things I can deal with, I live in the world after all, and the world is full of odd ideas.

But as he struggled, he became increasingly ad hominem. I am all for the shotgun approach but he exposed a deep, personal and bitter well. He launched into an embarrassing Facebook rant and deleted me. I suppose in today's etiquette this is like a slap with a glove and demand of satisfaction, for pistols or swords at dawn in the chateau grounds. He was one of a minority of soldiers and ex-soldiers I have met who couldn't quite get it – he bought the propaganda wholesale. After all, these military types are mostly very practical thinkers. I hold him no ill will, but our distance from each other is a sad thing because he was my brother when I was on the run and lost at the arse end of the world. He is very bright and also likes to write and I am quite sure one day he will write books about his awful politics and we can resume debates – which I will continue to win.

After a few weeks I got a package from the army resettlement service thanking me for my efforts and giving me career advice. I had already chosen to be an anti-imperialist activist by then. They had provided first-rate training for that. Also in the package was a bizarre little pin – like a Blue Peter badge – which said 'Veteran – HM Armed Forces'. I found it amusing that they had gifted me such a thing and I examined it for days, putting it on, taking it off, and sometimes wearing it in an attempt at irony. It seemed a strange parting gift after all that had passed and a break-up that had been particularly fraught. I eventually handed it back in to Downing Street by way of protest and got a letter from some administrative lackey telling me that it did not signify a particular operation and they were happy to send me another one if I wanted to wear my badge in the future.

I re-entered a real world beyond the green limits of the army. I spoke at meetings, gave lectures, took phone calls from some of the lads still in prison – mocking them, as promised, from the pub with a pint in my hand – did interviews for documentary makers and a few TV channels. The world was different somehow. My application to university had gone through and I would start be starting in September 2010.

It was a strange, disjointed time. The war carried on far away and deaths mounted. Afghanistan had been largely cut out of the public discourse except when there was a massacre or similar event which couldn't be ignored, and this remains the case. Though this was only after WikiLeaks had come to prominence with its lists and logs, and then it all died down again. This organization came from nowhere and stunned everyone. It is one of my greatest regrets that they came out too late for us to showcase at my trial. If we'd had those files earlier the trial would have been a perfect time to cite them.

Another soldier was locked up over it. Bradley Manning, a half-Welsh US Army intelligence analyst, was snatched for allegedly leaking masses of data and allowing the crimes in Afghanistan, Iraq and other places to be laid bare. Authorities have accused him of giving succour to the enemy and he is surely guilty of that. The enemy they are referring to is us – the ones who have been lied to and are paying the bill.

I would refer anyone considering joining the military to view the video of an Apache crew casually – even jovially – mowing down journalists and children in Iraq. That is the War on Terror. And everyone involved was a part of the crime: the technicians who maintained the helicopter, the armourers who fitted the guns, the pilots, the politicians who sent them and those boys who despatched every whistling bullet and every bang to the frontlines.

I do not have to have seen rounds hit or gape at the smoking ruins to be accountable. Those of us in the army were told daily where the bullets went. I am no longer an idiot according to the Ancient Greeks. These things do not happen in isolation, they are part of a long chain of conscious wrongdoing. This is not the plastic ethics of the politically powerful – this is just an explanation of the business of war. The military are the first people to talk about team-work, to talk about each of us as links in the chain and about how everyone must fulfil their little role. Presumably, so we can kill journalists and children and terrorists without differentiation.

Not long after that, another young serviceman refused to fight. He was a navy medic on submarines. However, he had been chosen to deploy to Afghanistan and he refused. Having seen WikiLeaks, he had acted on his conscience. He refused rifle training for operations. A petty officer later quoted in the press said that he was not teaching the sailor to go to war, only to fire a rifle. This is the Sailor Box – keeping everything compartmentalized much like the Soldier Box, a little military Narnian world, though presumably wetter. Given that the lad was being trained to wield that rifle in a war, rather than shoot ducks, he was well within his rights to refuse. He was further disturbed by being told that he could not attend to wounded Afghans, only to Western casualties. This went against his ethics as a healer.

He was actually allowed to go through the process of objection – a privilege which I was denied – and be heard by a panel of 'experts' only to be told that because he was secular his objections could not be moral, only political. A navy chaplain was involved in this decision – how very Christian of them. So atheists cannot have a moral position. They court-martialled him and he got eight months. He is a brave sailor, brave as they come. I would want people like that in my armed forces.

Clearly, even if I had been allowed to go before this conscientious objection board, my claims would likely have been rejected. Even if the board didn't reject claims for political reasons, then by not being religious I cannot have a conscience either. With that in mind I am glad I did it my own way, on my own terms. I later read that there was talk of this objection board being cut on the basis that we have a professional army, one of volunteers.

The only time there won't be a need for a conscientious objection board is when Britain somehow de-ratifies the laws that make conscientious objection a simple, legal right and, more importantly, when soldiers stop having consciences.

The only fall-back the military has is the same fatuous argument that armies put forward the world over: they say the floodgates will open and that we must be punished to deter the others. They said this to me, to all the American guys I know, the Israelis, the Turks, everyone. We all know these rivers might well break their banks given a chance. The difference is that some of us want to see it – we wish and work for it and we know it would be wholesome.

I'd been out of prison and the army a year when I met Ferret in Leeds one day. He was far too bright to stay in the army and was now a long-distance trucker. He had been passing through. He had two kids and was unfulfilled by his job but safer than before. He had put on weight sitting behind the wheel of a truck all day and he looked different to how he had in the desert, years before. We drank together and reminisced like old soldiers do, about harder, sandier times when we had no beer and we were leaner and fiercer. We mainly remembered the good stuff. We did this by agreeing on how shit all that good stuff had been, how cold it had been, how much we had hated it all and how much of a cunt nearly everyone was.

This is what soldiers do.

Chapter 21

University began and my course proved to be very good, although as soon as I started, it came under attack by the government. I paid a lot of tax during my time in Afghanistan and I'd rather it went on education than back into the wars. I was lucky to get into university before tuition fees were made crippling. The financial sector needed the money it had gambled away and so it was decided that we all would pay. The student revolt emerged from nowhere, and through this I got more and more involved in activism and the British left where the clamour is very loud and I try to contribute to the shouting.

A couple of the young men on my international relations course wanted to join the army and I debated them when I could. They reminded me of me: young, rash and unimaginative. They would go off to become commissioned officers – so effectively they were joining a very different army to me, the NCO – but I wanted to save them the hatred of their men. They were both good guys and it stung me to think of them wasted out there, though it was looking likely we wouldn't be in Afghanistan by the time they graduated. Things were going badly out there, bad enough that the media had been forced to start talking about it again. There were references to the Afghan My Lai moment: sixteen dead, apparently murdered by US soldiers at a place named Panjwai. But that was loose talk – there have been many My Lai moments in Afghanistan. So many that they might arguably have merged into one single My Lai moment, which has lasted for eleven years. All that is needed is a Tet moment, and that appears to have manifested in the growing trend of insider attacks – the killing of occupying troops by their native Afghan levies.

As I write, we have passed 430 dead servicemen and women in Afghanistan. However, there is no accurate tally for the Afghan dead. These deaths – all of them – were for naught. It disrespects them to just parrot the official line. It honours them to ask why they died and how we can avoid deaths like these in the future. I say this because I knew one or two of them.

After I left prison, I spoke at many meetings and when I was asked to do one in Bolton I hoped to meet the Second World War bomber crewman Hubert Lewis who had sent me such a powerful letter in prison. I arrived late to find an ex-soldier had turned up to the meeting in his regimental blazer. During the Q&A he kept chipping in trying to berate me or trip me up. He told me that there is an obligation to your mates, which is specific to the army and is sacred, and I had broken it. I told him that the idea of it being sacred was one he had borrowed or been told, that obligations like that are not specific to any institution, they are human. I explained that the bond is indeed special, though sacred sounded a little inflated, and there was no point in having it at all if you were going to let people squander it in a dirty war – that was a vile thing to do. I was opposing it, while he was approving of it. I managed to level his arguments. By then I had debated these issues so often and heard all the shit arguments he was regurgitating. Perhaps he sensed this; he excused himself and was heading for the hills by my last flourish. In the end though, he said he understood and that it was fair to do what I had done. I thanked him.

Afterwards I spoke to someone who had known Hubert Lewis and he said that the ex-bomber crewman would have liked to have heard and met me. They said he had been against war since those days he had spent bombing Europe. He'd died a few weeks earlier.

Although the wars — or ending them — will always be my passion, this single issue cannot be separated from others. At meetings people would not just talk to me about Afghanistan but about Palestine, Iraq, Kashmir, green politics, women's rights and much more. I knew so little back then, but the more I dug the more I became engaged in the wider political issues. All of these, it became apparent, could be traced to the same system. The wars, for example, were not anomalous, not a misapplication of the Western liberal ideas — this is how the world is arranged for us. Sadly, the wonderful, radical and worthy things about liberalism — which are numerous — seem to have died. John's prison lessons about freedom, class and equality were my grounding. I wasn't really new to these ideas as they had been present throughout my whole life, but they'd only become obvious in my struggle against the war.

The war went on, and working-class kids kept on dying, while the cheerleaders kept waving their pom-poms. I started to see more patterns emerging: particularly the one of denial, justification and the assigning and re-assigning of blame. Every time an atrocity was perpetrated — a Granai-style bombing, an Abu Ghraib, a Bagram, kill teams posing dead bodies for laughs and happy snaps, a Fallujah, a Baha Mousa, Marines peeing on dead Afghans, soldiers posing with SS flags, a Panjwai massacre — the excuses were always the same. It was some combination of bad apples, soldiers under severe stress, exceptional circumstances and collateral damage.

But these atrocities were not a case of humanitarian intervention being executed poorly, or a few bad soldiers. This is imperialism doing what imperialism does – killing people, destroying things, taking their stuff, trying to subjugate them. Imperial armies used to plunder cities and rape women and cannonade mutinous sepoys and now we have kill teams and drones and water-boarding and Guantanamo Bay. I guess some people would call this progress or civilization.

Beyond that, I wouldn't trust the people who created these wars with my life and I would not trust them with my family – a husband, a daughter, a son. It's a weird world when the man shooting rockets or bullets at you is not your worst enemy. He's just angry you're in his country – he's seen this all before. It's the people behind you that should be a concern – especially the ones a long way behind you. In fact, how far behind you they are could be directly proportional to the threat they pose to you. The enemy is all the way back there – probably in the direction your plane came from, back over all this sand, rock and earth. Their arguments – when simplified – seem to follow a pattern of logic rather like this: *We must be right, because if we are wrong then that means you are right and that cannot be allowed. That's virtually impossible, we couldn't even consider it. It's just not possible, is it?*

Chapter 22

The military's threats amounted to them throwing tantrums and they could not break me. They said you cannot change your mind. But you can and I did. They said to me that contracts are everything and should not be reneged upon. I used to make something of contracts, I now realize they are worthless unless they actually bind the parties equally. In reality, the world is in flux and contracts like that count for little and I never owed and never will owe the army's hierarchy or the government anything – not a thing. They, however, owe me and all the rest of us.

My mother bit back her grief over one son to look to another. So far I have not grieved properly. I would like to bury all this, but it is true. I still remember James as he lived, and this book is one of his memorials. He was unlike me; he was a gentler soul.

My own politics have gone from zero to very distinct and I do not pretend that I can divorce politics from the world around me anymore. I am still told that the society I live in is liberal and democratic and that this is 'lucky' and that I should be thankful that I don't live somewhere awful like Afghanistan. What they forget to tell you it that Afghanistan is as awful as it is today *because* of the actions of 'democracies'. Whatever may have been liberal or democratic about liberal democracy seems to have died in the wars it started. This is not lucky at all. The fact is liberal democracy makes a poor case for itself by militarizing young men and women in the name of security or progress and sending them to kill people just like themselves for profit, or influence or whatever. This is the Civilian Box. After all, my government put me away for refusing to help dominate and kill people.

The anti-war movement in Britain remains the apple of my eye and I cannot ever repay the efforts and support of all those people, who worked so hard for so many years before Lance Corporal Glenton blundered onto a stage at a meeting in London.

I met an overwhelming number of good souls who wanted to change the world in a profound way and have the determination to do it. I also discovered that even the best and most coherent political groups are in thrall to some unchecked egotism. Any soldier coming into contact with some of these setups would recognize it from their time in the military, a lot of bold people, as well as whichever petty foot-stamper who can shout the loudest flourishing at the expense of the troops. Sadly, as things stand, beasting is out of the question in the Revolutionary Box.

After a brief spell in and around these groups, I realized that having my name on a flyer for a meeting or demonstration was the priority. More averse to being treated like a mug than ever before, I realised I was being used as a 'name' and as part of the toxic celebrity culture that infects the left and is often justified under the guise of 'leadership'. For me, this phenomenon is itself an odd reflection of the mainstream. Likewise, as the political mainstream has been atomised into the bitty politics of race, gender, orientation, eye colour, bra size and so on, the left has allowed a particularly toxic version of identity politics creep in when a boot heel is the best remedy. Rather than social class, which unites vast numbers, the focus creeps onto these half-cocked politics of division. My card-carrying membership of the organized revolutionary left ended much as my relationship to the military had, on another one of those troublesome, damned points of principle. In the end, I chose to be as involved as I could in politics rather than the vacuous pantomime of a progressive force knocked off its bearing by twee, middling leftists trying to build what amounts (in my admittedly crude soldier's eye) to a knocking shop for geeks. It would be dishonest of me to suggest this kind of thing is limited to a particular sect or even that it is the major brake on progress, but it is a problem. I have a nose for that kind of thing, one remnant of my time as a lowly soldier being a lingering aversion to bullshit. Now I am an independent rebel, I'll work with anyone going my way and my politics and my knowledge of the landscape have been vastly improved for it.

How could I not have become a rebel? The whole episode was written through with issues of class, alienation, power and money – and all in the context of imperialism. It's hardly surprising that leftist arguments resonated with me, or mine with them and it's much better than being the pawn of imperialists.

I did what I thought was right in a given situation, and at times I'd like to be a grey man again, even to be just a soldier. I would be a lot more discerning in my choice of wars. My first instinct over Libya was to look for something akin to the international brigades of Civil War Spain. That was before the West hijacked that embryonic revolution and sponsored a set of pliable 'democrats' plucked from the ranks of the old regime and al-Qaeda. It was also before logic kicked in and I remembered I had no weapons and about two words of Arabic. I still want to act upon the world, I realized, though preferably through peaceful means. The twenty-two-year-old would-be soldier who wanted hardship and thought study

would be dull is still there, he's just older and a bit more measured. I have learned that it is right to take sides, it is folly to
wait endlessly for win-wins that cannot come; by doing so
you add to the deadweight of history. That's a game for the
flaky liberal, something I am not.

My journey continues. I am thirty as I finish this book – I
have been and remain poor, I've been homeless over and over
again, in care, war, exile and prison and I have no regrets. Jail
is a badge of honour: I will never have to explain to anyone
that I just went along with the war because 'it was my job'.
That would be uncomfortable. I stood and I fought and I did
my bit. That is to say I didn't go back to Afghanistan.

I recall all the bad things I have done – blamed stuff on
my brother when we were kids, tried to steal that car, I have
hated, drunk excessively, hit people in bars, cherished my
grudges (and still believe it right to do so) and said things
I shouldn't have, as well as all of my daily, human failures.
However, my refusal to return to Afghanistan, and my fight
regarding it, would not be among these. If nothing else it was
my rightest act. I am in the clear for that one, at least. I served
a jail term to prove it. But like my soldier friends I still have
sand in my eyes, we all have it there and it chafes our souls. It
recalls that place, that time and those lies.

Acknowledgments

I owe thanks to Leo Hollis and Verso, to my barrister, Nick Wrack, and the eminent John Tipple, to crass northern funny man Dr Owen Clayton and platinum Gellhorn Tansy Hoskins, to my family and friends for their support and to *mi revolucionaria tranquila*, Josephine Gough. I am grateful for the support and activism of the anti-war movement world-wide and the Stop the War Coalition in the UK. Thank you to the airmen, sailors and soldiers – serving and retired – who supported me because, in their words, 'The whole thing's bollocks anyway.' Finally thanks to the upper echelons of the military for being utterly inept, for buttressing my arguments, for giving me succour, teaching me to be bloody-minded and for setting me up with an unexpected and rewarding second career as a writer, filmmaker and informed, anti-imperialist thorn.